100 Interview Questions
GIT

X.Y. Wang

Contents

Chapter 1

Introduction

As the software development industry continues to evolve, the importance of version control systems in managing complex projects cannot be overstated. Git, a widely adopted distributed version control system, has become the go-to choice for developers and organizations around the world. It offers flexibility, efficiency, and security in managing source code and other digital assets. As a Git user, understanding its inner workings and mastering its features is essential to fully harness its power and reap its benefits in your development workflow.

"100 Interview Questions: GIT" aims to provide a comprehensive guide to Git, covering a wide range of topics from basic to advanced concepts. Whether you are a beginner looking to gain a solid foundation, an intermediate user ready to enhance your Git skills, or an expert seeking in-depth knowledge, this book has something for everyone. The questions and answers are designed to prepare you for interviews, equip you with the right knowledge to tackle real-world challenges, and help you become a more efficient and effective Git user.

The book is divided into five levels of proficiency: Basic, Intermediate, Advanced, Expert, and Guru. Each level covers a range of topics, starting with fundamental concepts and progressing to more complex and specialized subjects.

In the Basic section, you will find answers to common questions about Git, its purpose, and core functionalities. The Intermediate section delves into more advanced topics, such as branching, merging, and repository management. The Advanced section focuses on the Git object model, internal storage, and more sophisticated techniques for working with Git. The Expert section explores the inner workings of Git, including its algorithms, performance optimization, and integration with other systems. Finally, the Guru section discusses large-scale Git management, advanced conflict resolution, and best practices for Git usage in geographically distributed teams.

This book is designed to be a valuable resource for software developers, project managers, and anyone interested in learning more about Git. By the end of the book, you will have gained a deep understanding of Git, its features, and best practices, which will enable you to confidently navigate and excel in the world of software development.

Chapter 2

Basic

2.1 What is Git?

Git is a version control system that allows developers to manage changes to their codebase over time. It was created in 2005 by Linus Torvalds, the creator of Linux, and has since become one of the most widely used version control systems in the world.

Git is designed to be distributed, which means that every developer working on a project has a complete copy of the codebase, including the entire history of changes. This allows developers to work on their own copy of the codebase without interfering with each other, and to easily share their changes with others when they're ready.

One of the key features of Git is its ability to track changes to files over time. Each time a developer makes a change to a file, Git records the changes as a commit, along with a message describing what was changed. These commits are then organized into branches, which allow developers to work on different versions of the codebase simultaneously.

Git also includes features for managing conflicts that arise when multiple developers make changes to the same file. When conflicts occur, Git provides tools for resolving them and merging the changes together.

Finally, Git includes features for collaborating with other developers, including the ability to push and pull changes to and from remote repositories, as well as tools for reviewing and commenting on changes made by other developers.

Here is an example of how Git can be used in practice:

Suppose you're working on a team that is developing a web application. You've just been assigned a new feature to work on, and you want to start making changes to the codebase.

First, you would create a new branch in Git to work on your changes. This would allow you to make changes to the codebase without interfering with the work being done by other developers.

```
git checkout -b my-feature-branch
```

Next, you would make changes to the codebase to implement your new feature. As you make changes, you would use Git to track your progress, making commits along the way with messages describing what was changed.

```
git add .
git commit -m "Add new feature to web application"
```

Once you've finished making your changes, you would push them to a remote repository so that other developers on your team can review and comment on them.

```
git push origin my-feature-branch
```

Finally, once your changes have been reviewed and approved, you would merge them back into the main branch of the codebase so that they become part of the official version of the application.

```
git checkout main
git merge my-feature-branch
```

This is just a simple example of how Git can be used. In practice, Git can be used to manage much more complex codebases with multiple developers working on many different features simultaneously.

2.2 What is version control, and why is it important?

Version control is a system that allows developers to track changes to their code over time. It provides a way to manage multiple versions of a codebase, allowing developers to easily collaborate on a project, track changes made by different team members, and revert to earlier versions of the code if necessary.

Version control systems (VCS) like Git, SVN, and Mercurial are used to manage the source code of software projects. VCS keep a history of all changes made to the codebase, including who made the change, when it was made, and what was changed. This means that developers can keep track of how the codebase has evolved over time, and can easily see the differences between different versions of the code.

There are several reasons why version control is important in software development:

Collaboration: Version control systems allow developers to work on the same codebase simultaneously without interfering with each other. Each developer can make changes to their own copy of the codebase, and the changes can be merged together later. This allows multiple developers to work on the same project at the same time, which can speed up development and improve productivity.

History and recovery: Version control systems keep a complete history of changes made to the codebase, including who made the change, when it was made, and what was changed. This means that if something goes wrong, developers can easily revert to an earlier version of the code. This can be helpful if a bug is introduced, or if a feature is implemented incorrectly.

Code review: Version control systems provide a way for developers to review and comment on each other's code. Developers can review changes made by other team members before they are merged into the main codebase. This can help catch mistakes and improve the quality of the code.

Experimentation: Version control systems allow developers to create new branches of the codebase, which can be used to experiment with new features or changes. If the changes don't work out, they can be discarded without affecting the main codebase.

Here is an example of how version control can be used in practice:

Suppose you're working on a team that is developing a web application. You've just been assigned a new feature to work on, and you want to start making changes to the codebase.

First, you would create a new branch in your version control system to work on your changes. This would allow you to make changes to the codebase without interfering with the work being done by other developers.

```
git checkout -b my-feature-branch
```

Next, you would make changes to the codebase to implement your new feature. As you make changes, you would use your version control system to track your progress, making commits along the way with messages describing what was changed.

Once you've finished making your changes, you would push them to a remote repository so that other developers on your team can review and comment on them.

Finally, once your changes have been reviewed and approved, you would merge them back into the main branch of the codebase so that they become part of the official version of the application.

This is just a simple example of how version control can be used. In practice, version control is an essential tool for managing complex software projects with multiple developers working on many different features simultaneously.

2.3 Can you explain the difference between centralized and distributed version control systems?

Centralized version control systems (CVCS) and distributed version control systems (DVCS) are two types of version control systems that are commonly used in software development.

A centralized version control system, such as Subversion (SVN), is a system in which there is a single central repository that stores all versions of the codebase. Each developer has a local copy of the codebase on their own machine, but they must connect to the central repository to check out files, make changes, and commit changes back to the repository. In a CVCS, there is only one version of the codebase that exists at any given time, and developers must coordinate with each other to avoid conflicts.

In contrast, a distributed version control system, such as Git, is a system in which each developer has their own copy of the entire codebase, including all versions of the code. Each developer can work on their own copy of the codebase, and changes can be merged together later. In a DVCS, there are multiple versions of the codebase that exist simultaneously, and developers can work independently without coordinating with each other.

Here are some of the key differences between centralized and distributed version control systems:

Repository structure: In a CVCS, there is a single central repository that stores all versions of the codebase. In a DVCS, each developer has their own copy of the entire codebase, including all versions of the code.

Network dependency: In a CVCS, developers must be connected to the central repository to check out files, make changes, and commit changes back to the repository. In a DVCS, developers can work on their own copy of the codebase without being connected to a network, and changes can be merged together later.

Conflict resolution: In a CVCS, conflicts can occur when multiple developers make changes to the same file. Developers must coordinate with each other to avoid conflicts. In a DVCS, conflicts can also occur, but the system provides tools for resolving conflicts and merging changes together.

Branching and merging: In a CVCS, branching and merging can be more difficult and time-consuming because developers must coordinate with each other to avoid conflicts. In a DVCS, branching and merging are easier because each developer has their own copy of the codebase.

Here is an example of how a centralized version control system can be used in practice:

Suppose you're working on a team that is developing a web application. You've just been assigned a new feature to work on, and you want to start making changes to the codebase.

First, you would check out a copy of the codebase from the central repository.

```
svn checkout https://example.com/svn/my-project/
```

Next, you would make changes to the codebase to implement your new feature. As you make changes, you would use your version control system (Subversion) to track your progress, making commits along the way with messages describing what was changed.

```
svn add newfile.html
svn commit -m "Add new feature to web application"
```

Once you've finished making your changes, you would commit them back to the central repository so that other developers on your team can review and comment on them.

```
svn commit -m "Finished implementing new feature"
```

Finally, once your changes have been reviewed and approved, they would be merged into the main branch of the codebase so that they become part of the official version of the application.

```
svn update
svn merge my-feature-branch
svn commit -m "Merge my-feature-branch into main"
```

This is just a simple example of how a centralized version control system can be used. In practice, centralized version control systems can

2.4   How do you initialize a new Git repository?

To initialize a new Git repository, you need to perform the following steps:

Open a terminal or command prompt window. Navigate to the directory where you want to create the new Git repository. Run the git init command.

Here's an example of how to create a new Git repository:

Open a terminal window. Navigate to the directory where you want to create the new Git repository. For example, if you want to create a new repository in a directory called my-project, you would navigate to that directory using the cd command:

```
cd my-project
```

Run the git init command to initialize a new Git repository:

```
git init
```

After running this command, Git will create a new .git directory in your project directory. This directory contains all the files and metadata that Git uses to manage your project's version control.

At this point, your new Git repository is ready to use. You can start adding files to the repository, making commits, and branching the codebase as needed.

Here's an example of how to add a new file to the repository and make an initial commit:

Create a new file in your project directory. For example, create a file called README.md:

```
echo "# My Project" > README.md
```

Use the git add command to stage the new file for commit:

```
git add README.md
```

Use the git commit command to create a new commit with a message describing the changes you made:

```
git commit -m "Initial commit"
```

After running this command, Git will create a new commit with the changes you made to the README.md file. The commit will be stored in the repository's history, along with a message describing the changes you made.

That's it! You've now initialized a new Git repository and made an initial commit with some changes to the codebase. You can continue adding files and making commits to the repository as needed.

2.5 What is the purpose of the .gitignore file, and how do you create one?

The .gitignore file is a text file that specifies files and directories that Git should ignore when you commit changes to your repository. This can be useful for ignoring files that are automatically generated by your build process, temporary files, or sensitive files that you don't want to include in your repository.

When you create a .gitignore file in your repository, Git will use the rules specified in the file to determine which files to ignore. This can help keep your repository clean and focused on the files that are most important to your project.

Here's an example of how to create a .gitignore file:

Open a text editor such as Notepad, Sublime Text, or Atom.

Create a new file and name it .gitignore (note the leading dot).

Add the files and directories that you want to ignore to the file, one per line. For example, if you want to ignore all .log files and the node_modules directory, your .gitignore file might look like this:

```
*.log
node_modules/
```

Save the file in the root directory of your Git repository.

Once you've created your .gitignore file, Git will automatically ignore any files or directories that match the patterns specified in the file. This means that you can continue working on your project without worrying about accidentally committing files that you don't want to include in your repository.

Here are some additional tips for creating .gitignore files:

You can use wildcards to specify patterns of files to ignore. For example, *.log will ignore any files with the .log extension. You can use # to add comments to your .gitignore file. Anything after the # will be ignored by Git. You can create multiple .gitignore files in subdirectories of your repository to ignore files specific to those directories.

That's it! Now you know how to create a .gitignore file and how it can be used to help manage your Git repository.

2.6 What are the basic Git workflow stages?

Git follows a three-stage workflow when working with files in a repository. These stages are:

```
Working Directory
Staging Area (Index)
Repository (HEAD)
```

Here is a brief description of each stage:

Working Directory: This is the stage where you make changes to the files in your project. Any changes you make to files in this stage are not yet tracked by Git.

Staging Area (Index): This is the stage where you prepare your changes for a commit. You can use the git add command to add changes from the working directory to the staging area. Once you've added your changes to the staging area, they are ready to be committed to the repository.

Repository (HEAD): This is the stage where your changes are stored as commits in the Git repository. Once you've committed your changes, they become part of the repository's history and can be viewed and tracked by other developers.

Here's an example of how the Git workflow stages work in practice:

Working Directory: Suppose you have a file called index.html in your project directory, and you make changes to the file by adding some new content. These changes are made in the working directory and are not yet tracked by Git.

Staging Area (Index): To prepare your changes for a commit, you use the git add command to add the changes to the staging area:

```
git add index.html
```

This command adds the changes you made to index.html to the staging area.

Repository (HEAD): Finally, you use the git commit command to commit your changes to the repository:

```
git commit -m "Add new content to index.html"
```

This command creates a new commit with your changes and adds it to the repository's history.

In summary, the Git workflow stages are a key part of the Git version control system. By understanding how changes move through the working directory, staging area, and repository, you can effectively manage your codebase and track changes over time.

2.7 What is the difference between 'git add' and 'git commit' commands?

In Git, the git add and git commit commands are two separate commands that serve different purposes in the version control process.

git add is used to add changes made to files in the working directory to the staging area. The staging area is a temporary area where you can prepare your changes before committing them to the repository. When you run the git add command, Git will take a snapshot of the changes you've made to the files in the working directory and add them to the staging area.

Here's an example of how to use the git add command:

```
# Add all changes in the working directory to the staging area
git add .
```

Add specific files to the staging area git add file1.txt file2.html

git commit, on the other hand, is used to create a new commit with the changes that you've added to the staging area. A commit is a permanent snapshot of the changes made to the files in the repository. When you run the git commit command, Git will create a new commit with the changes you've added to the staging area, along with a commit message describing the changes.

Here's an example of how to use the git commit command:

```
# Create a new commit with the changes in the staging area
git commit -m "Add new feature to web application"
```

In summary, the git add command is used to add changes to the staging area, while the git commit command is used to create a new commit with the changes that have been added to the staging area. By using these two commands together, you can effectively manage changes to your codebase and keep track of the history of your project.

2.8 Can you explain the difference between 'git fetch' and 'git pull'?

In Git, git fetch and git pull are both commands that are used to update a local Git repository with changes from a remote repository. However, there are some important differences between the two commands.

git fetch is used to retrieve changes from a remote repository but does not merge those changes into your local repository. When you run the git fetch command, Git will download the latest changes from the remote repository and update your local copy of the remote branch. However, your local working copy and branch will remain unchanged.

Here's an example of how to use the git fetch command:

```
# Fetch changes from the remote repository
git fetch
```

After running this command, you can use other Git commands, such as git diff or git log, to compare the changes between your local and remote repositories. If you're satisfied with the changes, you can then use the git merge command to merge the changes into your local repository.

git pull, on the other hand, is used to retrieve changes from a remote repository and merge those changes into your local repository in one step. When you run the git pull command, Git will fetch the latest changes from the remote repository and automatically merge them into your local working copy.

Here's an example of how to use the git pull command:

```
# Pull changes from the remote repository and merge them into the local branch
git pull
```

In summary, the main difference between git fetch and git pull is that git fetch only retrieves changes from the remote repository, while git pull retrieves changes and merges them into your local repository in one step. If you want to review changes before merging them into your local repository, use git fetch and then use other Git commands to review the changes. If you're confident that you want to merge the changes into your local repository, use git pull to retrieve and merge the changes in one step.

2.9 What is a branch in Git, and how do you create one?

In Git, a branch is a separate line of development that allows you to work on new features or changes to your codebase without affecting the main codebase. Branches can be used to experiment with new ideas, fix bugs, or make major changes to the codebase without disrupting the main development workflow.

To create a new branch in Git, you can use the git branch command followed by the name of the new branch. Here's an example of how to create a new branch:

```
# Create a new branch called "new-feature"
git branch new-feature
```

After running this command, you will have a new branch called "new-feature". However, you will still be working on the original branch. To switch to the new branch, you can use the git checkout command:

```
# Switch to the new "new-feature" branch
git checkout new-feature
```

After running this command, you will be switched to the "new-feature" branch, and any changes you make to files in your repository will be made on the new branch.

Alternatively, you can create a new branch and switch to it in one step by using the git checkout command with the -b option:

```
# Create and switch to a new branch called "new-feature"
git checkout -b new-feature
```

This command will create a new branch called "new-feature" and switch to it in one step.

Once you've created a new branch, you can make changes to the files in your repository as usual. Any changes you make on the new branch will be isolated from the main codebase until you merge the changes back into the main branch.

In summary, branches are a powerful feature of Git that allow you to experiment with new features or changes to your codebase without affecting the main codebase. You can create a new branch using the git branch command and switch to it using the git checkout command. Alternatively, you can create and switch to a new branch in one step using the git checkout -b command.

2.10 How do you switch between branches in Git?

In Git, switching between branches is a common operation when working with multiple lines of development in a codebase. To switch between branches, you can use the git checkout command.

Here's an example of how to switch to an existing branch:

```
# Switch to an existing branch called "new-feature"
git checkout new-feature
```

After running this command, you will be switched to the "new-feature" branch. Any changes you make to files in your repository will be made on this branch.

If you want to create a new branch and switch to it in one step, you can use the -b option with the git checkout command:

```
# Create and switch to a new branch called "new-feature"
git checkout -b new-feature
```

After running this command, you will be switched to the new "new-feature" branch, and any changes you make to files in your repository will be made on this branch.

To list all branches in your repository, you can use the git branch command:

```
# List all branches in the repository
git branch
```

This command will show a list of all branches in your repository, with the current branch highlighted with an asterisk (*).

In summary, switching between branches in Git is a simple and common operation when working with multiple lines of development. To switch to an existing branch, use the git checkout command followed by the name of the branch. To create and switch to a new branch in one step, use the -b option with the git checkout command. You can list all branches in your repository using the git branch command.

2.11 What is the purpose of 'git merge', and how do you use it?

In Git, git merge is a command used to combine changes from different branches. The purpose of git merge is to integrate changes made on a branch into another branch, usually the main branch of the repository.

Here's an example of how to use the git merge command:

Suppose you have a branch called new-feature where you have made some changes to the codebase. You want to merge those changes into the main branch called master. Here's what you would do:

Switch to the branch that you want to merge the changes into. In this case, you would switch to the master branch:

```
git checkout master
```

Use the git merge command to merge the changes from the new-feature branch into the master branch:

```
git merge new-feature
```

After running this command, Git will automatically merge the changes from the new-feature branch into the master branch. If there are any conflicts between the two branches, Git will prompt you to resolve those conflicts before proceeding with the merge.

In addition to the basic merge operation, there are several options you can use with the git merge command to customize the merge behavior. For example, you can use the –no-ff option to create a merge commit even if the merge can be fast-forwarded:

```
git merge --no-ff new-feature
```

This option can be useful for creating a clear history of your repository's development.

In summary, git merge is a powerful command that allows you to combine changes from different branches in a Git repository. To use git merge, switch to the branch that you want to merge the changes into and use the git merge command with the name of the branch you want to merge. You can also use options with the git merge command to customize the merge behavior.

2.12   What is a 'git rebase', and when would you use it?

In Git, git rebase is a command used to modify the history of a branch. The purpose of git rebase is to move the changes from one branch to another, effectively rewriting the history of the branch.

Here's an example of how to use the git rebase command:

Suppose you have a branch called new-feature where you have made some changes to the codebase. You want to move those changes to the master branch. Here's what you would do:

Switch to the branch that you want to move the changes into. In this case, you would switch to the master branch:

```
git checkout master
```

Use the git rebase command to move the changes from the new-feature branch onto the master branch:

```
git rebase new-feature
```

After running this command, Git will reapply the changes from the new-feature branch onto the master branch, effectively rewriting the history of the master branch.

One common use case for git rebase is to integrate changes from a feature branch into the main branch of the repository. By using git rebase instead of git merge, you can keep the commit history of the feature branch separate from the main branch, resulting in a cleaner and more readable history.

Here's an example of how to use git rebase to integrate changes from a feature branch into the main branch:

```
# Create a new feature branch called "new-feature"
git checkout -b new-feature

# Make some changes on the new feature branch
...

# Switch back to the main branch
git checkout master

# Use git rebase to integrate the changes from the new feature branch into the
    main branch
git rebase new-feature
```

In summary, git rebase is a powerful command that allows you to move changes from one branch to another, effectively rewriting the history of a branch. You can use git rebase to integrate changes from a feature branch into the main branch of a repository while keeping the commit history clean and readable.

2.13   Can you explain the difference between 'git stash' and 'git stash apply'?

In Git, git stash and git stash apply are commands used to temporarily save changes in a Git repository. However, there are some important differences between the two commands.

git stash is used to save changes that are not ready to be committed, but you don't want to lose them either. When you run the git stash command, Git will save your changes in a temporary storage area called the stash. The stash is like a stack, so you can stash changes multiple times, and each time you stash, the new stash becomes the top of the stack.

Here's an example of how to use the git stash command:

```
# Stash changes that are not ready to be committed
git stash
```

After running this command, Git will save your changes in the stash.

git stash apply, on the other hand, is used to retrieve changes that you've saved in the stash and apply them to your working copy. When you run the git stash apply command, Git will apply the most recent stash to your working copy.

Here's an example of how to use the git stash apply command:

```
# Apply the most recent stash to your working copy
git stash apply
```

If you have multiple stashes, you can apply a specific stash by specifying its index:

```
# Apply the second stash to your working copy
git stash apply stash@{1}
```

In summary, git stash is used to temporarily save changes that are not ready to be committed, and git stash apply is used to retrieve changes from the stash and apply them to your working copy. By using these two commands, you can save changes that you don't want to commit yet but don't want to lose either, and retrieve them later when you're ready to continue working on them.

2.14   How do you view the commit history in Git?

In Git, you can view the commit history of a repository using the git log command. The git log command shows a chronological list of all the commits made in a repository, starting with the most recent commit.

Here's an example of how to use the git log command:

```
# View the commit history of the current branch
git log
```

This command will show a list of all the commits in the current branch, starting with the most recent commit. By default, the git log command shows each commit's SHA-1 hash, the author, the commit date, and the commit message.

You can also use options with the git log command to customize the output. For example, you can use the –pretty option to format the output of the git log command:

```
# View the commit history of the current branch with a custom format
git log --pretty=format:"%h - %an, %ar : %s"
```

This command will show a list of all the commits in the current branch, with a custom format that includes the commit hash, the author's name, the commit date in a relative format, and the commit message.

In addition to the git log command, there are several other commands you can use to view the commit history of a repository. For example, you can use the git show command to view the details of a specific commit:

```
# View the details of a specific commit
git show <commit-hash>
```

This command will show the details of the commit, including the commit message, the changes made in the commit, and the author.

In summary, you can view the commit history of a Git repository using the git log command. This command shows a chronological list of all the commits made in a repository. You can customize the output of the git log command using options such as –pretty. Additionally, you can use the git show command to view the details of a specific commit.

2.15 What is the purpose of the 'git remote' command, and how do you use it?

In Git, the git remote command is used to manage remote repositories. A remote repository is a copy of a Git repository that is hosted on a remote server, such as GitHub or GitLab. The purpose of the git remote command is to allow you to manage the remote repositories that your local repository interacts with.

Here's an example of how to use the git remote command:

```
# List all the remote repositories associated with your local repository
git remote -v
```

This command will show a list of all the remote repositories associated with your local repository, including their names and URLs.

You can also use the git remote add command to add a new remote repository to your local repository:

```
# Add a new remote repository called "origin"
git remote add origin git@github.com:username/repo.git
```

This command will add a new remote repository called "origin" to your local repository, with the URL git@github.com:username/repo.git.

Once you have added a remote repository to your local repository, you can use the git push and git pull commands to interact with the remote repository. For example, you can use the git push command to push changes from your local repository to the remote repository:

```
# Push changes from your local repository to the remote repository
git push origin master
```

This command will push the changes in your local repository's master branch to the remote repository called "origin".

In summary, the git remote command is used to manage remote repositories in Git. You can use the git remote command to list all the remote repositories associated with your local repository, add a new remote repository, and interact with remote repositories using commands like git push and git pull.

2.16   How do you clone a repository in Git?

In Git, you can clone a repository to make a local copy of the repository on your computer. Cloning a repository is useful if you want to contribute to an existing project or work on a project with multiple collaborators.

Here's an example of how to clone a repository in Git:

```
# Clone a repository from GitHub
git clone https://github.com/username/repo.git
```

This command will create a new directory called "repo" in your current directory and download a copy of the repository from GitHub into that directory.

You can also specify a directory name to use for the cloned repository:

```
# Clone a repository from GitHub into a directory called "my-project"
git clone https://github.com/username/repo.git my-project
```

This command will create a new directory called "my-project" in your current directory and download a copy of the repository from GitHub into that directory.

If the repository is hosted on a different server, you may need to specify a different URL to clone the repository. For example, if the repository is hosted on a GitLab server, you would use a URL like git@gitlab.com:username/repo.git instead of the GitHub URL shown in the examples above.

In summary, cloning a repository in Git is a simple process that allows you to make a local copy of a repository on your computer. To clone a repository, use the git clone command followed by the URL of the repository you want to clone. You can also specify a directory name to use for the cloned repository.

2.17 How do you create and apply a patch in Git?

In Git, a patch is a file that contains the differences between two commits or between a commit and your working copy. Patches are useful for sharing changes with other developers who may not have access to your Git repository or for applying changes to a different copy of a repository.

Here's an example of how to create a patch in Git:

```
\# Create a patch that contains the changes in the most recent commit
git format-patch HEAD^
```

This command will create a patch file that contains the changes in the most recent commit. The HEADârgument specifies the commit to create the patch from.

You can also create a patch that contains the changes between two commits:

```
# Create a patch that contains the changes between two commits
git format-patch <commit1>..<commit2>
```

This command will create a patch file that contains the changes between the two specified commits.

Once you have created a patch, you can apply it using the git apply command:

```
# Apply a patch file to your working copy
git apply path/to/patch/file
```

This command will apply the changes in the patch file to your working copy. If there are any conflicts between the patch and your working copy, Git will prompt you to resolve those conflicts before proceeding with the patch.

In addition to the git apply command, there is also a git am command that can be used to apply patches. The git am command is designed to apply patches that were created using the git format-patch command.

In summary, creating and applying patches in Git is a useful way to share changes with other developers or apply changes to a different copy of a repository. To create a patch, use the git format-patch command, and to apply a patch, use the git apply or git am command.

2.18 What is the purpose of 'git revert' and 'git reset', and what are the differences between them?

In Git, git revert and git reset are two commands that can be used to undo changes in a Git repository. However, they have different purposes and should be used in different situations.

git revert is used to undo a commit by creating a new commit that undoes the changes made in the original commit. When you run the git revert command, Git will create a new commit that contains the inverse of the changes made in the original commit.

Here's an example of how to use the git revert command:

```
# Undo the changes made in a specific commit
git revert <commit-hash>
```

This command will create a new commit that undoes the changes made in the specified commit.

git reset, on the other hand, is used to undo changes by resetting the current branch to a previous commit. When you run the git reset command, Git will move the current branch pointer to the specified commit and discard any changes made after that commit.

Here's an example of how to use the git reset command:

```
# Undo the changes made after a specific commit
git reset <commit-hash>
```

This command will move the current branch pointer to the specified commit and discard any changes made after that commit.

One key difference between git revert and git reset is that git revert creates a new commit that undoes the changes made in the original commit, while git reset discards the changes made after the specified commit.

Another difference is that git revert can be used to undo changes that have already been pushed to a remote repository, while git reset should not be used to undo changes that have been pushed to a remote repository, as it can cause problems for other developers who have pulled those changes.

In summary, git revert and git reset are two commands used to undo changes in a Git repository. git revert is used to create a new commit that undoes the changes made in a previous commit, while git reset is used to move the current branch pointer to a previous commit and discard any changes made after that commit. It is important to use these commands correctly to avoid causing problems for other developers or losing important changes.

2.19   How do you resolve merge conflicts in Git?

In Git, a merge conflict occurs when Git is unable to automatically merge changes from two or more branches. This can happen when two or more branches have made changes to the same file or lines of code.

Here's an example of how to resolve a merge conflict in Git:

Start by running the git status command to see which files have merge conflicts:

```
# Check which files have merge conflicts
git status
```

Open the file with the merge conflict in a text editor. You will see that Git has marked the conflicting lines with «««<, =======, and »»»> markers. The lines between «««< and ======= represent the changes from the current branch, while the lines between ======= and »»»> represent the changes from the branch being merged.

```
<<<<<<< HEAD
This is the text from the current branch.
=======
This is the text from the branch being merged.
>>>>>>> branch-to-merge
```

Edit the file to resolve the conflict. You can keep one set of changes, or merge the changes together. Once you have resolved the conflict, remove the «««<, =======, and »»»> markers from the file.

```
This is the text from both branches.
```

Once you have resolved all the merge conflicts, stage the changes using the git add command:

```
# Stage the changes
git add <filename>
```

Finally, commit the changes using the git commit command:

```
# Commit the changes
git commit -m "Merge branch-to-merge"
```

This will commit the changes to the repository and complete the merge.

In summary, resolving merge conflicts in Git requires manually editing the conflicting file to resolve the differences between the two branches. Once the conflicts have been resolved, the changes must be staged and committed to complete the merge.

2.20 What are the best practices for writing a good commit message?

Writing a good commit message is important for making it easy to understand the changes made in a commit and to provide context for other developers who may be working on the same project. Here are some best practices for writing a good commit message in Git:

Keep the message concise and descriptive: A commit message should be brief but informative. It should describe the changes made in the commit in a way that is easy to understand.

Use the imperative mood: A commit message should be written in the imperative mood, which means it should be written as if giving a command. For example, instead of saying "Changed the file," say "Change the file."

Separate the subject from the body: A commit message should be divided into two parts: a subject and a body. The subject should be a short summary of the changes made in the commit, while the body should provide more details about the changes.

Provide context: A commit message should provide context for the changes made in the commit. This can include information about why the changes were made, what problem they solved, or any relevant information about the project or feature being worked on.

Use the present tense: A commit message should be written in the present tense, as if describing the changes being made at the time of the commit. For example, instead of saying "Changed the file," say "Change the file."

Here's an example of a good commit message:

```
Add feature to sort list of items
```

This commit adds a new feature to sort a list of items by name or date. The feature is accessed through the context menu by right-clicking on a list item. Sorting is performed using a stable sorting algorithm to ensure that items with the same name or date remain in their original order.

In summary, writing a good commit message in Git involves keeping the message concise and descriptive, using the imperative mood, separating the subject from the body, providing context, and using the present tense. Following these best practices can make it easier to understand the changes made in a commit and to provide context for other developers working on the project.

Chapter 3

Intermediate

3.1 What is the difference between a "fast-forward" and a "recursive" merge in Git?

In Git, a merge is used to combine changes from two or more branches into a single branch. There are two types of merges in Git: fast-forward and recursive.

A fast-forward merge occurs when the branch being merged has all of its changes in a straight line from the current branch. In other words, there are no changes on the current branch that are not already on the branch being merged. When a fast-forward merge occurs, Git simply moves the current branch pointer to the commit of the branch being merged.

Here's an example of a fast-forward merge:

```
# Create a new branch called "feature"
git branch feature

# Switch to the "feature" branch
git checkout feature

# Make changes and commit them
echo "Some changes" > file.txt
git add file.txt
git commit -m "Add changes"

# Switch back to the main branch
git checkout main

# Merge the changes from the "feature" branch
git merge feature
```

In this example, the git merge command will perform a fast-forward merge, since the changes made in the "feature" branch are already in a straight line from the current branch.

A recursive merge, on the other hand, occurs when the branch being merged has changes that are not already in a straight line from the current branch. When a recursive merge occurs, Git will create a new commit that combines the changes from both branches.

Here's an example of a recursive merge:

```
# Create a new branch called "feature"
git branch feature

# Switch to the "feature" branch
git checkout feature

# Make changes and commit them
echo "Some changes" > file.txt
git add file.txt
git commit -m "Add changes"

# Switch back to the main branch
git checkout main

# Make changes and commit them
echo "More changes" > file.txt
git add file.txt
git commit -m "Add more changes"

# Merge the changes from the "feature" branch
git merge feature
```

In this example, the git merge command will perform a recursive merge, since there are changes on both the "main" and "feature" branches that are not in a straight line from each other.

In summary, a fast-forward merge occurs when the branch being merged has all of its changes in a straight line from the current branch, while a recursive merge occurs when the branch being merged has changes that are not in a straight line from the current branch. Understanding the difference between these two types of merges can help you choose the right merge strategy for your project.

3.2 How can you view the differences between the working directory and the most recent commit?

In Git, you can view the differences between the working directory and the most recent commit using the git diff command. The git diff command compares the current state of the files in your working directory to the most recent commit and shows the differences between them.

Here's an example of how to use the git diff command:

```
# View the differences between the working directory and the most recent
    commit
git diff
```

This command will show the differences between the files in your working directory and the most recent commit. Lines that have been added to the file will be shown in green, while lines that have been removed will be shown in red.

If you want to see the differences between a specific file in your working directory and the most recent commit, you can specify the file name as an argument to the git diff command:

```
# View the differences between a specific file in the working directory and
    the most recent commit
git diff <file-name>
```

This command will show the differences between the specified file in your working directory and the most recent commit.

In summary, you can view the differences between the working directory and the most recent commit using the git diff command. This command compares the current state of the files in your working directory to the most recent commit and shows the differences between them. By using the git diff command, you can easily see what changes have been made since the last commit, which can be helpful for reviewing changes before committing them or debugging issues in your code.

3.3 How do you remove untracked files from your working directory?

In Git, untracked files are files that are not part of the repository and have not been added to the staging area. If you want to remove untracked files from your working directory, you can use the git clean command. The git clean command removes untracked files from the working directory.

Before running the git clean command, it's a good idea to check which files will be removed. You can use the -n or –dry-run option to do this:

```
# Dry run to see which files will be removed
git clean -n
```

This command will show you a list of untracked files that will be removed if you run the git clean command.

To remove untracked files from the working directory, use the -f or –force option with the git clean command:

```
# Remove untracked files from the working directory
git clean -f
```

This command will remove all untracked files from the working directory.

If you want to remove untracked directories as well as files, use the -d option:

```
# Remove untracked directories as well as files
git clean -fd
```

This command will remove all untracked files and directories from the working directory.

It's important to note that the git clean command permanently deletes files and directories, so make sure you really want to delete them before running this command.

In summary, you can remove untracked files from your working directory in Git using the git clean command with the -f or –force option. The git clean command permanently deletes files and directories, so use it with caution.

3.4 What is a detached HEAD in Git, and how do you deal with it?

In Git, a "detached HEAD" state occurs when you checkout a specific commit or tag instead of a branch. In this state, the HEAD pointer (which points to the current branch) is not pointing to a branch, but to a specific commit.

Here's an example of how to enter a detached HEAD state in Git:

```
# Checkout a specific commit
git checkout <commit-hash>
```

In this example, the git checkout command is used to checkout a specific commit. This will put Git into a detached HEAD state.

While in a detached HEAD state, you can still make changes to the code and commit those changes. However, if you create a new commit while in this state, you will not be on a branch and the changes will not be part of any branch.

To deal with a detached HEAD state, you can either create a new branch at the current commit or switch back to an existing branch. Here's how to create a new branch:

```
# Create a new branch at the current commit
git branch <new-branch-name>
```

This will create a new branch at the current commit and put you back on a branch. You can now continue making changes and committing them as normal.

To switch back to an existing branch, use the git checkout command followed by the name of the branch:

```
# Switch back to an existing branch
git checkout <branch-name>
```

This will switch you back to the specified branch and put you in a "normal" state where you can continue making changes and committing them.

In summary, a detached HEAD state in Git occurs when you checkout a specific commit instead of a branch. While in this state, you can still make changes and commit them, but those changes will not be part of any branch. To deal with a detached HEAD state, you can either create a new branch at the current commit or switch back to an existing branch.

3.5   How do you use 'git bisect' to find a specific commit that introduced a bug?

In Git, the git bisect command is a useful tool for identifying the commit that introduced a bug or regression. The git bisect command works by performing a binary search on the commit history, allowing you to quickly narrow down the commit that introduced the bug.

Here's how to use git bisect to find a specific commit that introduced a bug:

Start by checking out a known good commit, usually the latest stable release or a commit that you know does not contain the bug.

```
# Checkout a known good commit
git checkout <good-commit>
```

Start the bisect process using the git bisect start command.

```
# Start the bisect process
git bisect start
```

Mark the current commit as "bad" by running the git bisect bad command.

```
# Mark the current commit as "bad"
git bisect bad
```

Mark an older commit as "good" by running the git bisect good command. This should be a commit that you know does not contain the bug.

```
# Mark an older commit as "good"
git bisect good <older-good-commit>
```

Git will automatically checkout a new commit in between the "good" and "bad" commits, and prompt you to test the code and determine whether the bug is present or not. Mark the commit as "good" or "bad" using the git bisect good or git bisect bad command, respectively.

```
# Test the code and mark the commit as "good" or "bad"
git bisect good   # if the code works as expected
git bisect bad    # if the bug is present
```

Repeat step 5 until Git has identified the specific commit that introduced the bug. Once Git has identified the commit, it will print out the commit hash and information about the commit.

```
# Repeat step 5 until Git has identified the commit that introduced the bug
git bisect good/bad
```

Once the commit has been identified, Git will print out the commit hash and information

Finish the bisect process using the git bisect reset command to return to the original state.

```
# Finish the bisect process
git bisect reset
```

In summary, the git bisect command is a powerful tool for identifying the commit that introduced a bug or regression in Git. By performing a binary search on the commit history, git bisect allows you to quickly narrow down the commit that introduced the bug, and can save you a lot of time and effort in the debugging process.

3.6 What is the purpose of 'git cherry-pick', and how do you use it?

In Git, the git cherry-pick command is used to apply the changes introduced by a specific commit to another branch. This can be useful when you want to selectively apply changes from one branch to another, without merging the entire branch.

Here's how to use git cherry-pick:

Identify the commit that contains the changes you want to apply to another branch. You can use the git log command to view the commit history.

```
# View the commit history
git log
```

Checkout the branch that you want to apply the changes to.

```
# Checkout the target branch
git checkout <target-branch>
```

Use the git cherry-pick command followed by the commit hash of the commit you want to apply. This will apply the changes introduced by the commit to the current branch.

```
# Cherry-pick a specific commit
git cherry-pick <commit-hash>
```

Alternatively, you can cherry-pick a range of commits by specifying a range of commit hashes.

```
# Cherry-pick a range of commits
git cherry-pick <start-commit-hash>..<end-commit-hash>
```

Resolve any conflicts that may arise during the cherry-pick process. If the changes in the target branch conflict with the changes introduced by the cherry-picked commit, Git will pause the cherry-pick process and prompt you to resolve the conflicts manually.

```
# Resolve conflicts
git mergetool   # opens the mergetool to resolve conflicts
git add <file>  # stage the resolved conflicts
git cherry-pick --continue  # continue the cherry-pick process
```

Once all conflicts have been resolved, commit the changes using the git commit command.

```
# Commit the changes
git commit
```

In summary, the git cherry-pick command is used to apply the changes introduced by a specific commit to another branch. By using git cherry-pick, you can selectively apply changes from one branch to another, without merging the entire branch. This can be useful when you want to apply a bug fix or feature from one branch to another, or when you need to apply changes from a historical commit to a current branch.

3.7 How do you use 'git reflog', and when would you need it?

In Git, the git reflog command is used to view a log of changes to the repository's references, including the branch and HEAD pointers. The git reflog command is useful for recovering lost commits or branches, as well as for troubleshooting issues with the repository's history.

Here's how to use git reflog:

Open a Git repository in your terminal and run the following command:

```
# View the Git reflog
git reflog
```

This will display a list of the recent changes to the repository's references, including the branch and HEAD pointers.

Identify the commit or branch that you want to recover. The git reflog output will include the commit hashes for each change, as well as the branch or HEAD pointer associated with the change.

Use the git checkout command to checkout the desired commit or branch.

```
# Checkout a commit or branch
git checkout <commit-hash or branch-name>
```

Alternatively, you can use the git reset command to reset the current branch to the desired commit or branch.

```
# Reset the current branch to a commit or branch
git reset --hard <commit-hash or branch-name>
```

Once you have recovered the desired commit or branch, you can continue working with the repository as usual.

The git reflog command is especially useful in situations where you have accidentally deleted a branch or committed changes that you did not intend to. By reviewing the git reflog output, you can identify the lost branch or commit and recover it easily.

In summary, the git reflog command is used to view a log of changes to the repository's references, including the branch and HEAD pointers. It can be useful for recovering lost commits or branches, as well as for troubleshooting issues with the repository's history.

3.8 Can you explain the difference between a shallow clone and a deep clone in Git?

In Git, a shallow clone and a deep clone refer to the depth of the commit history that is copied during the cloning process.

A shallow clone is a Git clone that only copies a limited number of commits from the remote repository. By default, Git clones the entire commit history of the remote repository. However, with a shallow clone, you can limit the depth of the commit history that is copied, resulting in a smaller repository size and a faster cloning process.

Here's an example of how to create a shallow clone:

```
# Create a shallow clone of a remote repository
git clone --depth=1 <remote-repository-url>
```

In this example, the –depth option limits the depth of the cloned history to only the most recent commit.

A deep clone, on the other hand, is a Git clone that copies the entire commit history of the remote repository. This is the default behavior of the git clone command.

Here's an example of how to create a deep clone:

```
# Create a deep clone of a remote repository
git clone <remote-repository-url>
```

In summary, a shallow clone is a Git clone that only copies a limited number of commits from the remote repository, while a deep clone copies the entire commit history of the remote repository. Shallow clones can be useful when you only need the most recent commits, as they result in a smaller repository size and a faster cloning process. However, deep clones are necessary when you need access to the entire commit history of the remote repository.

3.9 How do you create and use Git aliases to simplify your workflow?

In Git, aliases are shortcuts that you can create to simplify commonly used Git commands. By using aliases, you can save time and reduce the amount of typing required to execute Git commands. Git aliases can be created for any Git command, as well as for custom scripts and commands.

Here's how to create a Git alias:

Open your Git configuration file in your text editor:

```
git config --global --edit
```

This command will open the Git configuration file in your default text editor.

Add the alias to the [alias] section of the file, using the following format:

```
[alias]
<alias-name> = <git-command>
```

For example, to create an alias for the git status command, you can add the following line to the configuration file:

```
[alias]
st = status
```

Save and close the file.

Once you have created an alias, you can use it in place of the original Git command. For example, to use the st alias to execute the git status command, you would enter the following in your terminal:

```
git st
```

In addition to creating aliases for Git commands, you can also create aliases for custom scripts and commands. For example, you can create an alias for a script that runs a suite of tests, or for a command that deploys your code to a production server.

Here's an example of how to create an alias for a custom script:

Create a script and save it to a location in your file system. For example, you can create a script called run-tests.sh that runs a suite of tests.

Open your Git configuration file in your text editor:

```
git config --global --edit
```

Add the alias to the [alias] section of the file, using the following format:

```
[alias]
<alias-name> = !<command>
```

For example, to create an alias for the run-tests.sh script, you can add the following line to the configuration file:

```
[alias]
test = !sh /path/to/run-tests.sh
```

Save and close the file.

Once you have created an alias for your custom script, you can use it in place of the original Git command. For example, to use the test alias to execute the run-tests.sh script, you would enter the following in your terminal:

```
git test
```

In summary, Git aliases are shortcuts that you can create to simplify commonly used Git commands. By using aliases, you can save time and reduce the amount of typing required to execute Git commands. You can create aliases for any Git command, as well as for custom scripts and commands. Git aliases can be created and managed in the Git configuration file.

3.10   What are Git submodules, and how do you use them?

In Git, submodules are a way to include one Git repository inside another Git repository. This is useful when you want to include external dependencies in your project, or when you want to reuse code across multiple projects.

Here's how to add a submodule to your Git repository:

Open your Git repository in your terminal.

Use the git submodule add command to add a submodule to your repository:

```
# Add a submodule to your Git repository
git submodule add <submodule-url> <submodule-path>
```

In this command, <submodule-url> is the URL of the Git repository that you want to include as a submodule, and <submodule-path> is the path where you want to store the submodule within your repository.

Commit the changes to your repository:

```
# Commit the submodule changes to your Git repository
git commit -m "Added submodule"
```

Now that you have added a submodule to your Git repository, you can use it in your project as you would any other directory. However, you should keep in mind that the submodule is a separate Git repository, and any changes made to the submodule will need to be committed and pushed separately from the parent repository.

Here are some common commands that you can use to work with submodules:

git submodule init: Initializes the submodules in your repository.

git submodule update: Updates the submodules in your repository to their latest commit.

git submodule foreach: Executes a Git command in each submodule.

git submodule sync: Updates the URL of a submodule to match the URL in the .gitmodules file.

git submodule status: Displays the status of the submodules in your repository.

In summary, Git submodules are a way to include one Git repository inside another Git repository. They are useful when you want to include external dependencies in your project, or when you want to reuse code across multiple projects. Submodules can be added to your Git repository using the git sub-module add command, and can be managed using a variety of Git commands.

3.11 How do you squash multiple commits into a single commit using 'git rebase'?

In Git, squashing multiple commits into a single commit is a way to simplify the commit history of a branch. This is useful when you have made several small, incremental commits that can be combined into a single, cohesive commit.

Here's how to squash multiple commits into a single commit using git rebase:

Open your Git repository in your terminal.

Use the git log command to view the commit history of your branch. Identify the commit that you want to keep as the base commit for your squashed commit. Note the commit hash for this commit.

Use the git rebase -i command to initiate an interactive rebase:

```
# Initiate an interactive rebase
git rebase -i <base-commit-hash>
```

In this command, <base-commit-hash> is the hash of the commit that you identified in step 2.

In the interactive rebase editor that opens, locate the commits that you want to squash. Change the word "pick" to "squash" or "s" for each commit that you want to squash.

```
# Interactive rebase editor
pick abc123 First commit
s def456 Second commit
s ghi789 Third commit
```

In this example, the second and third commits will be squashed into the first commit.

Save and close the interactive rebase editor.

In the next editor that opens, modify the commit message for your squashed commit. The commit message should describe the changes that were made in all of the squashed commits.

Save and close the commit message editor.

Use the git log command to verify that the squashed commit has been created.

Push your changes to the remote repository:

```
# Push the squashed commit to the remote repository
git push --force
```

In this command, the –force option is necessary because you have rewritten the Git history of your branch.

In summary, squashing multiple commits into a single commit using git rebase is a way to simplify the commit history of a branch. This can be done using an interactive rebase, where you specify the commits that you want to squash and modify the commit message for the squashed commit. After squashing the commits, you should verify the changes using git log and then push the changes to the remote repository using git push –force.

3.12 What is the purpose of 'git blame', and how do you use it?

In Git, git blame is a command that can be used to view the author and last modification time of each line in a file. This is useful for identifying who made changes to a file and when those changes were made.

Here's how to use git blame:

Open your Git repository in your terminal.

Use the git blame command followed by the path to the file that you want to view:

```
# View the git blame information for a file
git blame <file-path>
```

The output of the git blame command will display the commit hash, author name, and last modification time for each line in the file. For example:

```
abc1234 (John Smith 2022-03-18 13:00:00 +0800  1) This is the first line of
    the file
def5678 (Jane Doe 2022-03-19 14:00:00 +0800  2) This is the second line of the
    file
abc1234 (John Smith 2022-03-18 13:00:00 +0800  3) This is the third line of
    the file
```

In this example, the first and third lines of the file were last modified by John Smith on March 18, 2022, and the second line was last modified by Jane Doe on March 19, 2022.

Use the -L option followed by a range of line numbers to view the git blame information for a specific range of lines in the file. For example:

```
# View the git blame information for lines 3-5 of a file
git blame -L 3,5 <file-path>
```

In this command, -L 3,5 specifies that you want to view the git blame information for lines 3-5 of the file.

In summary, git blame is a command that can be used to view the author and last modification time of each line in a file. This is useful for identifying who made changes to a file and when those changes were made. You can use git blame followed by the path to the file to view the git blame information for the entire file, or you can use the -L option followed by a range of line numbers to view the git blame information for a specific range of lines in the file.

3.13   How do you sign your commits with GPG in Git, and why is it important?

In Git, signing your commits with GPG (GNU Privacy Guard) is a way to verify the authenticity of your commits. By signing your commits with GPG, you can provide assurance that the commit was made by you and has not been tampered with.

Here's how to sign your commits with GPG:

Install GPG on your computer if you haven't already done so.

Generate a GPG key:

```
# Generate a GPG key
gpg --gen-key
```

Configure Git to use your GPG key:

```
# Configure Git to use your GPG key
git config --global user.signingkey <key-id>
```

In this command, <key-id> is the ID of your GPG key. You can find the ID of your key using the gpg –list-keys command.

Commit your changes as usual:

```
# Commit your changes
git commit -m "Your commit message"
```

Use the -S or –gpg-sign option to sign your commit with GPG:

```
# Sign your commit with GPG
git commit -S -m "Your commit message"
```

In this command, the -S or –gpg-sign option tells Git to sign your commit with GPG.

Push your changes to the remote repository:

```
# Push your changes to the remote repository
git push
```

In summary, signing your commits with GPG in Git is a way to verify the authenticity of your commits. To sign your commits with GPG, you must first generate a GPG key and configure Git to use your key. After configuring Git, you can sign your commits with GPG using the -S or –gpg-sign option when committing your changes. It is important to sign your commits with GPG to provide assurance that the commit was made by you and has not been tampered with.

3.14   Can you explain the difference between 'git push –force' and 'git push –force-with-lease'?

In Git, git push –force and git push –force-with-lease are both commands that can be used to force-push changes to a remote repository. However, there is an important difference between these two commands.

git push –force overwrites the remote branch with your local branch, regardless of whether there have been any changes made to the remote branch since your last pull. This can be dangerous if you are collaborating with others, as it can result in the loss of their changes.

git push –force-with-lease, on the other hand, will only force-push changes to the remote branch if the remote branch matches the local branch. If there have been any changes made to the remote branch since your last pull, Git will reject the push and display an error message. This can help to prevent the loss of other collaborators' changes.

Here's an example to illustrate the difference between these two commands:

Alice and Bob both clone a Git repository and make changes to the same file.

Alice commits her changes and pushes them to the remote repository:

```
# Alice commits her changes and pushes them to the remote repository
git add <file>
git commit -m "Alice's changes"
git push
```

Bob also commits his changes and tries to push them to the remote repository using git push –force:

```
# Bob commits his changes and force-pushes them to the remote repository
git add <file>
git commit -m "Bob's changes"
git push --force
```

Because Bob used git push –force, his changes overwrite Alice's changes, resulting in the loss of Alice's work.

```
# Alice's changes are lost
git log
commit 1234 (HEAD -> master)
Author: Bob
Date:   2022-03-20 12:00:00 +0800

Bob's changes
```

If Bob had used git push –force-with-lease instead, Git would have detected that the remote branch had been updated since Bob's last pull and would have rejected the push. This would have prevented the loss of Alice's changes.

In summary, git push –force and git push –force-with-lease are both commands that can be used to force-push changes to a remote repository. However, git push –force overwrites the remote branch regardless of whether there have been any changes made to the remote branch since your last pull, while git push –force-with-lease will only force-push changes if the remote branch matches the local branch. It is generally recommended to use git push –force-with-lease to prevent the loss of other collaborators' changes.

3.15 How do you set up a Git hook, and what are some common use cases?

In Git, a hook is a script that is triggered by a certain Git event, such as committing or pushing changes. Git hooks can be used to automate certain tasks or to enforce rules and policies.

Here's how to set up a Git hook:

Navigate to the .git/hooks directory in your Git repository.

```
cd .git/hooks
```

Create a new file with the name of the hook you want to create (e.g., pre-commit, post-commit, pre-push, etc.). Make the file executable.

```
touch pre-commit
chmod +x pre-commit
```

Write the script for the hook. The script should be in Bash or another scripting language supported by your system. For example, a pre-commit hook might look like this:

```bash
#!/bin/bash

# Check for whitespace errors in the files being committed
git diff-index --check --cached HEAD
if [ $? != 0 ]; then
echo "Whitespace errors detected. Please fix them before committing."
exit 1
fi
```

Save the script and exit the file.

```
:wq
```

Now, every time you commit changes to your repository, the pre-commit hook will be executed. In this example, the hook checks for whitespace errors in the files being committed and exits with an error if any are found.

Some common use cases for Git hooks include:

Checking for syntax errors or code style violations before committing changes Running tests before committing changes Preventing certain files or directories from being committed Enforcing commit message formatting or content requirements Sending notifications or performing other actions after certain Git events occur

In summary, Git hooks are scripts that are triggered by certain Git events, such as committing or pushing changes. Git hooks can be used to automate tasks, enforce rules and policies, or perform other actions. To set up a Git hook, create a script in the .git/hooks directory and make it executable. Common use cases for Git hooks include checking for syntax errors, running tests, and enforcing commit message requirements.

3.16 How do you manage multiple remote repositories in a single local Git repository?

In Git, it's possible to manage multiple remote repositories in a single local repository. This can be useful when working on a project that has multiple remote repositories, such as a main repository and a forked repository.

Here's how to manage multiple remote repositories in Git:

Add the remote repositories to your local repository using the git remote add command. You can use any name you like for the remote repository (e.g., origin, upstream, forked, etc.).

```
git remote add origin git://github.com/user/repo.git
git remote add upstream git://github.com/otheruser/repo.git
git remote add forked git://github.com/myuser/repo.git
```

Verify that the remote repositories were added successfully using the git remote
-v command.

```
git remote -v
origin   git://github.com/user/repo.git (fetch)
origin   git://github.com/user/repo.git (push)
upstream git://github.com/otheruser/repo.git (fetch)
upstream git://github.com/otheruser/repo.git (push)
forked   git://github.com/myuser/repo.git (fetch)
forked   git://github.com/myuser/repo.git (push)
```

Push changes to the appropriate remote repository using the git push command
and the name of the remote repository.

```
# Push changes to the origin remote repository
git push origin master

# Push changes to the forked remote repository
git push forked mybranch
```

Pull changes from the appropriate remote repository using the git pull command
and the name of the remote repository.

```
# Pull changes from the upstream remote repository
git pull upstream master

# Pull changes from the forked remote repository
git pull forked mybranch
```

By default, Git will use the origin remote repository for push and pull operations. To push or pull changes to a different remote repository, you can specify
the name of the remote repository as an argument to the git push or git pull
command.

In summary, to manage multiple remote repositories in a single local Git repository, you can add the remote repositories using the git remote add command,
verify that they were added successfully using the git remote -v command, and
push or pull changes to the appropriate remote repository using the git push or
git pull command with the name of the remote repository.

3.17 What is the purpose of 'git tag', and how do you create and use tags in Git?

In Git, a tag is a way to mark a specific commit with a label. Tags can be used
to identify important milestones in a project's history, such as releases, and they
can be used to quickly reference specific commits.

Here's how to create and use tags in Git:

Create a tag for the current commit using the git tag command.

```
git tag v1.0.0
```

Verify that the tag was created successfully using the git tag command.

```
git tag
v1.0.0
```

Push the tag to the remote repository using the git push command with the –tags option.

```
git push --tags
```

Check out a specific tag using the git checkout command.

```
git checkout v1.0.0
```

This will switch your working directory to the commit that the tag points to.

Create an annotated tag with a message using the -a option and a message with the -m option.

```
git tag -a v1.1.0 -m "Release version 1.1.0"
```

An annotated tag includes a message that can provide additional context about the tag.

View the details of a specific tag using the git show command.

```
git show v1.1.0
```

This will display information about the commit that the tag points to, as well as the tag message (if the tag is annotated).

In summary, a tag is a way to mark a specific commit with a label in Git. Tags can be used to identify important milestones in a project's history, such as releases, and they can be used to quickly reference specific commits. To create a tag, use the git tag command, and to push the tag to the remote repository, use the git push command with the –tags option. To check out a specific tag, use the git checkout command, and to view the details of a specific tag, use the git show command.

3.18 How do you configure Git to use a specific text editor or diff tool?

By default, Git uses a built-in text editor (usually Vim or Emacs) for editing commit messages and other text files. However, you can configure Git to use a different text editor or diff tool of your choice.

Here's how to configure Git to use a specific text editor:

Set the core.editor configuration variable to the path of the text editor you want to use.

```
git config --global core.editor "nano"
```

This example sets the core.editor variable to use the Nano text editor.

Verify that the core.editor variable was set correctly using the git config command.

```
git config --global core.editor
nano
```

This example verifies that the core.editor variable is set to use the Nano text editor.

Here's how to configure Git to use a specific diff tool:

Set the diff.tool configuration variable to the name of the diff tool you want to use.

```
git config --global diff.tool "meld"
```

This example sets the diff.tool variable to use the Meld diff tool.

Set the difftool.prompt configuration variable to false to prevent Git from prompting you to confirm each diff.

```
git config --global difftool.prompt false
```

Verify that the diff.tool variable was set correctly using the git config command.

```
git config --global diff.tool
meld
```

This example verifies that the diff.tool variable is set to use the Meld diff tool.

Use the git difftool command to open the diff tool.

```
git difftool file.txt
```

This will open the Meld diff tool (in this example) to compare the changes in file.txt.

In summary, to configure Git to use a specific text editor, set the core.editor configuration variable to the path of the text editor you want to use. To configure Git to use a specific diff tool, set the diff.tool configuration variable to the name of the diff tool you want to use, and set the difftool.prompt variable to false to prevent Git from prompting you to confirm each diff. Then, use the git difftool command to open the diff tool.

3.19   How do you use 'git clean' to remove untracked files and directories?

The git clean command is used to remove untracked files and directories from the working directory. By default, git clean will only remove files that are not being tracked by Git, but you can also use options to remove directories or force the removal of files that are ignored by Git.

Here's how to use git clean to remove untracked files and directories:

View the untracked files and directories using the git status command.

```
git status
```

This will show you the files and directories that are not being tracked by Git.

Dry-run git clean to see which files and directories would be removed.

```
git clean -n
```

This will perform a dry-run of git clean, which means that it will show you which files and directories would be removed, but it won't actually remove them.

Remove untracked files and directories.

```
git clean -f
```

This will remove the untracked files and directories from the working directory.

You can use additional options with git clean to modify its behavior:

-d: Remove untracked directories in addition to files. -x: Remove untracked files and directories that are ignored by Git. -n: Perform a dry-run of git clean to see which files and directories would be removed. -f: Force the removal of files and directories, even if they are not writable or have merge conflicts.

In summary, git clean is used to remove untracked files and directories from the working directory. You can use additional options to remove directories, force the removal of ignored files, perform a dry-run, or force the removal of files and directories that have conflicts. Be careful when using git clean, as it can permanently delete files that you may not intend to remove. It's a good idea to perform a dry-run first to make sure that you know which files and directories will be removed.

3.20 What is a Git bare repository, and when would you use one?

A Git bare repository is a repository that doesn't have a working directory. Instead, it only contains the Git database (the .git directory) and the contents of the repository's branches. In other words, a bare repository is like the "master" copy of a repository, and it doesn't have a working copy that you can edit files in. Instead, it's designed to be used as a centralized repository that multiple developers can push and pull changes to and from.

Here's how to create a Git bare repository:

```
git init --bare /path/to/repository.git
```

This will create a new Git bare repository at the specified path. Note that the ".git" extension is usually added to the repository name to indicate that it's a bare repository.

Here are some common use cases for a Git bare repository:

Centralized team collaboration: A bare repository can be used as a central repository that multiple developers can push and pull changes to and from. This is a common workflow for teams working on a project together.

Backup repository: A bare repository can also be used as a backup repository that's kept on a remote server or in the cloud. This can be useful if you want to have a copy of your repository that's separate from your working copy.

Deploy repository: A bare repository can be used to deploy code to a production server or other location. This is a common workflow for web developers who want to push code changes to a remote server.

In summary, a Git bare repository is a repository that doesn't have a working directory, and it's used as a centralized repository for multiple developers to push and pull changes to and from. Bare repositories are also useful as backup repositories and deploy repositories. When creating a bare repository, make sure to add the ".git" extension to the repository name.

Chapter 4

Advanced

4.1 Can you explain the Git object model, including blobs, trees, and commits?

The Git object model is the underlying data structure that Git uses to store and manage the contents of a repository. It consists of three main types of objects: blobs, trees, and commits.

Blobs: A blob represents the contents of a file. Blobs are immutable objects, which means that they cannot be changed once they are created. When you make changes to a file, Git creates a new blob to represent the updated contents of the file.

Trees: A tree represents a directory in the repository. A tree object contains pointers to one or more blobs and/or other tree objects. When you create a new file or directory in the repository, Git creates a new tree object to represent the updated contents of the directory.

Commits: A commit represents a snapshot of the repository at a particular point in time. A commit contains metadata such as the author, date, and commit message, as well as a pointer to the tree object that represents the state of the repository at the time the commit was made. When you make a new commit, Git creates a new commit object that points to the tree object representing the updated repository state.

Here's a visual representation of the Git object model:

```
Commit
|
v
```

```
Tree <---- Blob
 |          |
 v          v
Tree       Blob
 |          |
 v          v
...        ...
```

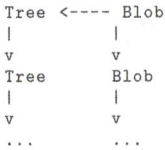

In this diagram, each arrow represents a pointer from one object to another. Commits point to trees, trees point to blobs (or other trees), and blobs represent the contents of files.

In summary, the Git object model is the underlying data structure that Git uses to store and manage the contents of a repository. Blobs represent file contents, trees represent directories, and commits represent snapshots of the repository at a particular point in time. By understanding the Git object model, you can gain a better understanding of how Git works and how to use it effectively.

4.2 How does Git store data internally, and what is the role of the Git object database?

Git stores data internally using its own unique data structure. When you add a file to Git, it creates a new blob object to represent the contents of the file. When you create a new directory, Git creates a new tree object to represent the directory's contents. When you make a new commit, Git creates a new commit object that points to the tree object representing the repository's state at the time of the commit.

All of these objects are stored in the Git object database, which is essentially a content-addressable key-value store. Each object is given a unique SHA-1 hash, which serves as its key in the database. The contents of the object are stored as a value associated with the key. When you reference an object in Git, you do so using its SHA-1 hash.

The Git object database is stored in the .git/objects directory of your repository. Each object is stored in a separate file in this directory, with the first two characters of the file name representing the first two characters of the object's SHA-1 hash. The remaining characters of the file name represent the rest of the object's SHA-1 hash.

Here's an example of how Git stores data internally:

```
echo "Hello, world" > hello.txt
git add hello.txt
git commit -m "Add hello.txt"
```

When you run these commands, Git creates a new blob object to represent the contents of hello.txt. It then creates a new tree object to represent the root directory of the repository, and adds a pointer to the blob object from the tree object. Finally, it creates a new commit object that points to the tree object.

All of these objects are stored in the Git object database. You can view the contents of the object database using the git cat-file command:

```
git cat-file -p <object-hash>
```

Where <object-hash> is the SHA-1 hash of the object you want to view.

In summary, Git stores data internally using its own unique data structure. Each object is given a unique SHA-1 hash and stored in the Git object database. The role of the Git object database is to provide a content-addressable key-value store for Git objects. By understanding how Git stores data internally, you can gain a better understanding of how Git works and how to use it effectively.

4.3   What are Git's packfiles, and how do they optimize repository storage?

Git's packfiles are a way of storing Git objects more efficiently in the Git object database. When you add files to a Git repository, Git creates a new object for each file, which can take up a significant amount of disk space over time. However, not all of these objects are equally important or frequently accessed. Some objects may be larger than others or have fewer connections to other objects.

To optimize the storage of these objects, Git uses a technique called delta compression. This involves finding objects that are similar to each other and storing only the differences between them. This can greatly reduce the amount of disk space needed to store a repository's objects.

Here's an example of how Git creates a packfile:

```
git gc
```

When you run this command, Git performs a garbage collection operation on the Git object database. This involves identifying any objects that are no longer needed (such as objects that are not referenced by any branch or tag), and removing them from the object database. Git also identifies any objects that can be packed together more efficiently, and packs them into a new packfile.

Packfiles are stored in the .git/objects/pack directory of your repository, and have a .pack extension. They are binary files that contain compressed Git objects, along with an index file that allows Git to quickly locate individual objects within the packfile.

By using packfiles, Git can greatly reduce the amount of disk space needed to store a repository's objects. It can also improve the performance of Git operations, as accessing a packed object is typically faster than accessing an unpacked object.

In summary, Git's packfiles are a way of storing Git objects more efficiently in the Git object database. They use delta compression to store only the differences between similar objects, which can greatly reduce the amount of disk space needed to store a repository's objects. By understanding how Git uses packfiles, you can gain a better understanding of how Git works and how to use it effectively.

4.4 Can you explain the concept of a "rebase conflict" and how to resolve it?

A "rebase conflict" occurs when you attempt to rebase a branch onto another branch, and Git encounters a change in the original branch that conflicts with a change in the branch being rebased. This can happen when two different changes modify the same file or the same lines of code within a file.

When a rebase conflict occurs, Git will pause the rebase process and inform you of the conflict. You will then need to resolve the conflict manually before the rebase process can continue.

Here's an example of how to resolve a rebase conflict:

Start the rebase process:

```
git checkout feature-branch
git rebase master
```

Git will pause the rebase process and inform you of the conflict. You can use the git status command to see which files have conflicts:

```
Unmerged paths:
(use "git add <file>..." to mark resolution)

both modified:   file.txt
```

Open the conflicted file(s) in your text editor and look for the conflict markers. These markers will indicate where the conflicting changes occurred:

```
<<<<<<< HEAD
This is the version of the file from the feature-branch.
=======
```

```
This is the version of the file from the master branch.
>>>>>>> master
```

Edit the file to resolve the conflict. You can either choose one version of the change or create a new version that combines both changes. Once you have resolved the conflict, save the file.

Use the git add command to stage the resolved file:

```
git add file.txt
```

Continue the rebase process:

```
git rebase --continue
```

If there are additional conflicts, repeat steps 3-6 until all conflicts have been resolved and the rebase process has completed.

It's important to note that a rebase conflict can be more complex than the example above, especially if multiple files or lines of code are in conflict. In some cases, you may need to manually edit the files to resolve the conflicts.

In summary, a rebase conflict occurs when Git encounters conflicting changes in the branch being rebased. To resolve a rebase conflict, you will need to manually edit the conflicted file(s) and choose which version of the change to keep. Once you have resolved the conflict, you can continue the rebase process.

4.5   How do you interact with Git's staging area without using 'git add' and 'git rm' commands?

To interact with Git's staging area without using the git add and git rm commands, you can use a combination of other Git commands and options that allow you to manipulate the staging area directly. Here are a few examples:

Use git reset to unstage changes:

```
git reset file.txt
```

This command will unstage any changes to the file file.txt that have been added to the staging area. The changes will remain in the working directory.

Use git rm --cached to remove files from the staging area:

```
git rm --cached file.txt
```

This command will remove the file file.txt from the staging area, but will leave it in the working directory.

Use git update-index to stage changes:

```
git update-index --add file.txt
```

This command will add the changes to the file file.txt to the staging area, but will leave them uncommitted. You can use git commit to commit the changes.

Use git add –patch to interactively stage changes:

```
git add --patch file.txt
```

This command will allow you to interactively stage changes to the file file.txt. Git will present you with a prompt for each change, allowing you to choose whether to stage it, skip it, or split it into smaller changes.

It's worth noting that while these commands allow you to interact with the staging area directly, they are not a replacement for git add and git rm. These commands are designed to be used together to give you fine-grained control over the changes you commit.

In summary, there are several Git commands and options that allow you to interact with the staging area without using git add and git rm. These commands include git reset, git rm –cached, git update-index, and git add –patch. While they can be useful in certain situations, they are not a replacement for the git add and git rm commands.

4.6   How do you split a repository into multiple smaller repositories while preserving history?

There are several scenarios where you may need to split a large Git repository into multiple smaller repositories while preserving the history. Here are a few methods you can use to accomplish this:

Use git filter-branch: This is a powerful and flexible tool that allows you to rewrite the history of a Git repository. One way to use git filter-branch to split a repository is to create a new branch that contains only the files you want to split off, and then use git filter-branch to remove all other files from the branch history.

```
# Create a new branch containing only the files to split off
git checkout -b new-branch
git filter-branch --subdirectory-filter path/to/files
```

```
# Create a new repository for the split-off files
mkdir new-repo
cd new-repo
git init
git pull /path/to/original-repo new-branch
```

This will create a new repository with only the files from the path/to/files directory and their full history.

Use git subtree: This is a Git extension that allows you to split a repository into multiple smaller repositories. You can use git subtree to extract a directory from the original repository into a new repository, while preserving the commit history.

```
# Create a new repository for the split-off files
git init new-repo
cd new-repo

# Extract the directory from the original repository into the new repository
git subtree split --prefix=path/to/files -b new-branch
git pull /path/to/original-repo new-branch
```

This will create a new repository with only the files from the path/to/files directory and their full history.

Use git clone: This method involves cloning the original repository and then removing the unwanted files from the cloned repository.

```
# Clone the original repository
git clone /path/to/original-repo new-repo
cd new-repo

# Remove the unwanted files from the cloned repository
git filter-branch --tree-filter 'rm -rf path/to/files' HEAD
```

This will remove the unwanted files from the cloned repository, while preserving the commit history.

In summary, there are several methods you can use to split a Git repository into multiple smaller repositories while preserving the history. These methods include using git filter-branch, git subtree, and git clone with git filter-branch. Each method has its own strengths and weaknesses, so you should choose the one that best fits your specific situation.

4.7 Can you describe the process of rebasing an entire branch onto another branch, including resolving conflicts?

Rebasing is the process of moving a branch to a new base commit. When rebasing an entire branch onto another branch, the idea is to take all the changes made on the source branch and apply them to the destination branch, as if they were made directly on top of it.

Here's an example of how to rebase a branch named "feature-branch" onto the "main" branch:

Ensure you are on the "main" branch by executing the following command:

```
git checkout main
```

Fetch the latest changes from the remote repository by executing the following command:

```
git fetch origin
```

Merge the latest changes from the "main" branch by executing the following command:

```
git merge origin/main
```

Switch back to the "feature-branch" branch by executing the following command:

```
git checkout feature-branch
```

Rebase the "feature-branch" branch onto the "main" branch by executing the following command:

```
git rebase main
```

This will take all the changes made on the "feature-branch" branch and apply them on top of the latest changes on the "main" branch.

If there are any conflicts during the rebase process, Git will pause the process and ask you to resolve them. You can use the following command to see which files have conflicts:

```
git status
```

You can then edit the conflicted files and resolve the conflicts manually. Once the conflicts are resolved, you can continue the rebase process by executing the following command:

```
git add .
git rebase --continue
```

This will stage the changes you made to resolve the conflicts and continue the rebase process.

Once the rebase is complete, you can push your changes to the remote repository by executing the following command:

```
git push --force-with-lease origin feature-branch
```

This will push your changes to the "feature-branch" branch on the remote repository.

In summary, rebasing an entire branch onto another branch involves switching to the destination branch, merging the latest changes, switching back to the source branch, and then rebasing the source branch onto the destination branch. During the rebase process, conflicts may arise, which must be resolved manually before continuing the rebase process. Once the rebase is complete, the changes can be pushed to the remote repository.

4.8 How do you use 'git filter-branch' or 'git filter-repo' to modify the history of a Git repository?

Both 'git filter-branch' and 'git filter-repo' are used to modify the history of a Git repository, but they work in slightly different ways.

Using 'git filter-branch'

'git filter-branch' is a built-in Git command that can be used to rewrite the history of a Git repository by applying a filter to each commit. This filter can be used to remove or modify files, change the author or committer information, or make any other changes to the commit history. The rewritten history can then be pushed to the remote repository, but it's important to note that this can cause issues for other contributors who have based their work on the original history.

Here's an example of how to use 'git filter-branch' to remove a file from the commit history:

Change to the root directory of the repository:

```
cd /path/to/repository
```

Backup the original repository in case something goes wrong:

```
git clone . ../backup-repo
```

Run the 'git filter-branch' command, specifying the filter to apply:

```
git filter-branch --tree-filter 'rm -f path/to/file' HEAD
```

This command removes the file located at "path/to/file" from all commits in the history. The '–tree-filter' option specifies a shell command to apply to each commit.

Push the modified history to the remote repository:

```
git push --force origin master
```

It's important to use the '–force' option to overwrite the remote history with the modified history.

Using 'git filter-repo'

'git filter-repo' is a newer, more powerful tool that was designed to replace 'git filter-branch'. It's faster, easier to use, and can perform more complex operations than 'git filter-branch'. It's also less likely to cause issues for other contributors, as it preserves the original commits by default.

Here's an example of how to use 'git filter-repo' to remove a file from the commit history:

Change to the root directory of the repository:

```
cd /path/to/repository
```

Install 'git filter-repo' if it's not already installed:

```
git clone https://github.com/newren/git-filter-repo
export PATH="$PWD/git-filter-repo:$PATH"
```

Backup the original repository in case something goes wrong:

```
git clone . ../backup-repo
```

Run the 'git filter-repo' command, specifying the filter to apply:

```
git filter-repo --path path/to/file
```

This command removes the file located at "path/to/file" from all commits in the history. The '–path' option specifies the file or directory to remove.

Push the modified history to the remote repository:

```
git push --force origin master
```

It's important to use the '–force' option to overwrite the remote history with the modified history.

In summary, 'git filter-branch' and 'git filter-repo' can be used to modify the history of a Git repository by applying a filter to each commit. 'git filter-branch' can be used to remove or modify files, change the author or committer information, or make any other changes to the commit history. 'git filter-repo' is a newer, more powerful tool that can perform more complex operations than 'git filter-branch', while preserving the original commits by default. However, it's important to use caution when modifying the history of a Git repository, as it can cause issues for other contributors who have based

4.9 How do you use 'git refspec' to configure advanced push and fetch behaviors?

In Git, a refspec is a string that defines the mapping between local and remote references. It is used to specify the source and destination references for Git push and fetch operations. A refspec can be used to configure advanced push and fetch behaviors, such as pushing a local branch to a remote branch with a different name or fetching only specific branches from a remote repository.

The basic syntax of a refspec is:

```
<source>:<destination>
```

where <source> and <destination> are references to commits or branches. Here are some examples:

Push a local branch to a remote branch with a different name:

```
git push origin local-branch:remote-branch
```

Delete a remote branch:

```
git push origin :remote-branch
```

Fetch only specific branches from a remote repository:

```
git fetch origin branch1 branch2
```

Fetch all remote branches and tags:

```
git fetch --all --tags
```

Fetch a single tag:

```
git fetch origin tagname
```

Fetch a specific commit:

```
git fetch origin <commit-hash>:<destination-branch>
```

It's important to note that refspecs can be quite powerful but can also be dangerous if not used carefully. It's always a good idea to double-check the refspecs before executing any push or fetch command. Additionally, some hosting services such as GitHub allow repository administrators to restrict the types of refspecs that can be used in order to prevent accidental data loss or corruption.

4.10 What is the Git garbage collection process, and when should it be run manually?

In Git, the garbage collection process is responsible for cleaning up unreferenced objects and optimizing the repository's storage. When an object in Git is no longer needed, such as a commit that has been replaced by a newer version, it becomes an "unreferenced object" and is a candidate for removal by the garbage collector.

Git's garbage collection process runs automatically in the background, but it can also be run manually using the git gc command. This command performs a number of operations to optimize the repository's storage, including:

Packing loose objects into packfiles for more efficient storage

Removing unreachable objects

Compressing objects to save space

Cleaning up unused reflogs

By default, Git runs the garbage collector automatically when certain conditions are met, such as when the repository reaches a certain size or when a certain number of objects have been added or removed. However, there are times when it may be necessary to run the garbage collector manually, such as when a large number of objects have been deleted or when disk space is running low.

To run the garbage collector manually, simply use the git gc command in the repository's root directory. You can also specify additional options to control the behavior of the garbage collector, such as the –aggressive option to perform more aggressive optimization or the –prune=now option to immediately remove all unreferenced objects.

It's worth noting that the garbage collector can be a resource-intensive process, especially for larger repositories. It's generally recommended to let Git handle garbage collection automatically, but if you do need to run it manually, be sure to monitor resource usage and give it enough time to complete without interrupting the process.

4.11 How do you configure a Git repository to use Large File Storage (LFS)?

Git Large File Storage (LFS) is an extension to Git that allows large files to be stored outside the main repository, thus reducing the size of the repository and improving performance. Here are the steps to configure a Git repository to use LFS:

Install Git LFS: First, you need to install Git LFS on your local machine. You can download and install Git LFS from the official website or by using a package manager like Homebrew or apt-get.

Initialize Git LFS: Once you have installed Git LFS, you need to initialize it for your repository. Run the following command in your repository's root directory:

```
git lfs install
```

This command sets up Git LFS for your repository and modifies your Git configuration to enable LFS tracking.

Choose file types to track: By default, Git LFS tracks files with extensions like .jpg, .png, and .pdf. However, you can customize the file types that Git LFS tracks by creating a .gitattributes file in your repository's root directory. For example, if you want to track files with a .psd extension, you can add the following line to your .gitattributes file:

```
*.psd filter=lfs diff=lfs merge=lfs -text
```

Track large files: Once you have configured Git LFS for your repository, you can start tracking large files by running the following command:

```
git lfs track "<pattern>"
```

Replace <pattern> with a file or a wildcard pattern that matches the files you want to track. For example, to track all .psd files, you can run:

```
git lfs track "*.psd"
```

Commit and push changes: After you have configured Git LFS and started tracking large files, you can commit and push your changes as usual. When you push changes that include large files, Git LFS will automatically upload the files to the LFS server and replace them with small text pointers in the main repository.

That's it! Now your Git repository is configured to use Git LFS for large files. When you clone the repository on another machine, Git LFS will automatically download the large files from the LFS server and replace the text pointers with the original files.

4.12 How do you use 'git rerere' to reuse resolved merge conflicts, and what are the potential risks?

Git rerere, short for "reuse recorded resolution," is a feature that allows Git to remember how you resolved merge conflicts in the past and reuse the same resolution for similar conflicts in the future. Here's how to use it:

Enable Git rerere: You can enable Git rerere by running the following command:

```
git config --global rerere.enabled true
```

This command tells Git to start recording merge resolutions in the .git/rr-cache directory.

Resolve a merge conflict: When you encounter a merge conflict, resolve it as you normally would using your preferred merge tool. Git rerere will automatically record your resolution and save it in the .git/rr-cache directory.

Test Git rerere: To test Git rerere, you can intentionally create a merge conflict and resolve it using the same resolution as before. Git rerere will automatically reuse the recorded resolution and apply it to the new conflict.

```
$ git merge feature-branch
Auto-merging myfile.txt
CONFLICT (content): Merge conflict in myfile.txt
Resolved 'myfile.txt' using previous resolution.
Automatic merge went well; stopped before committing as requested
```

In this example, Git rerere automatically resolved the merge conflict in myfile.txt using a previously recorded resolution.

Using Git rerere can save time and effort when dealing with recurring merge conflicts, but there are some potential risks to consider:

Misleading history: Rerere can reuse merge conflict resolutions, which may lead to a misleading history. For example, if a conflict resolution is incorrect, rerere may apply it to similar conflicts in the future, resulting in a history that appears correct but is actually wrong.

Confidential data: Rerere caches conflict resolutions in plain text, which may expose confidential data if the resolutions contain sensitive information.

Maintenance overhead: Rerere's cache needs to be maintained over time to avoid stale or invalid resolutions, which can add overhead to the repository's maintenance.

To mitigate these risks, it's important to review rerere's cache regularly and ensure that the recorded resolutions are correct and do not expose sensitive data. Additionally, rerere can be disabled on a per-repository basis by running the command git config rerere.enabled false.

4.13 What are some advanced techniques for searching Git commit history, such as using 'git log' with custom formats and filters?

When working with Git, the ability to search through commit history is a critical tool for tracking changes, identifying issues, and understanding the evolution of a project. There are several advanced techniques for searching Git commit history, and some of the most useful ones are:

Using custom formatting with 'git log': Git log can be customized to display a range of information about each commit, such as the author, commit message, date, and SHA-1 hash. By using custom formatting options, you can create detailed reports that provide insight into the history of the project. For example, the following command displays a list of commits in a condensed format that shows only the commit hash, author, and date:

```
git log --pretty=format:'%h %an %ad'
```

Using filters with 'git log': Git log can also be filtered to display only commits that match specific criteria. For example, you can use the '–grep' option to search for commits that contain a particular keyword in the commit message:

```
git log --grep='bugfix'
```

You can also filter by author, date range, file name, and other criteria.

Using 'git blame': Git blame is a command that displays the revision and author information for each line of a file. This can be useful for identifying who made changes to a specific section of code and when those changes were made. For example, the following command shows the author and revision information for each line of the 'app.js' file:

```
git blame app.js
```

Using 'git bisect': Git bisect is a command that helps you find the commit that introduced a bug by performing a binary search through the commit history. You start by identifying a "good" commit (one that does not have the bug) and a "bad" commit (one that does have the bug), and Git bisect checks out a middle commit between the two. You then test the code at that commit and tell Git whether it is "good" or "bad." Git bisect repeats the process, halving the number of possible commits with each iteration, until it identifies the commit that introduced the bug.

Overall, using these advanced search techniques can help you gain a deeper understanding of the history of a Git repository and more effectively manage changes and issues.

4.14   Can you explain the purpose of 'git notes', and how do you use them?

Git notes are a way to attach additional information or annotations to a Git commit without modifying the commit itself. This can be useful for adding context or metadata to a commit, such as tracking issue numbers or recording review comments.

To create a note for a commit, you can use the git notes add command followed by the commit hash:

```
git notes add <commit-hash>
```

This will open your default text editor, allowing you to enter the note content. Once you save and close the editor, the note will be created and associated with the specified commit.

To view the notes for a particular commit, you can use the git notes show command:

```
git notes show <commit-hash>
```

By default, this will display the notes in your terminal. You can also use the –ref option to specify a particular notes ref (which defaults to refs/notes/commits) if you have multiple notes refs in your repository.

You can also edit or delete existing notes using the git notes edit and git notes remove commands, respectively.

One important thing to note (no pun intended) is that notes are not included in the default output of commands like git log. To include notes in the output, you can use the –show-notes option:

```
git log --show-notes=<notes-ref>
```

This will display the notes for each commit in addition to the normal log output.

Overall, Git notes can be a powerful tool for adding extra information to your commit history in a non-destructive way. However, they should be used judiciously and with care, as they can add complexity and potential confusion to your repository if overused.

4.15 How do you implement a custom merge strategy in Git?

Git comes with a variety of built-in merge strategies for combining changes from multiple branches, such as the default recursive strategy, as well as more specialized strategies like ours and subtree. However, there may be cases where none of these built-in strategies are suitable for your needs, and you need to implement a custom merge strategy.

A custom merge strategy in Git is implemented as a script that takes three arguments: the merge base commit, the current branch tip commit, and the other branch tip commit. The script must produce a new commit that represents the merged state of the two branches, and exit with a status code of 0 if the merge was successful, or a non-zero status code if the merge failed.

Here's an example of a simple custom merge strategy that always chooses the changes from the current branch:

```bash
#!/bin/bash

# Get the merge base commit, current branch tip, and other branch tip
base="$1"
ours="$2"
theirs="$3"

# Create a new tree that includes all the changes from the current branch
tree=$(git merge-tree "$base" "$ours" "$theirs" | sed 's/    /t/g')

# Create a new commit with the merged tree
commit=$(echo "Merge branch 'ours' into 'theirs'" | git commit-tree "$tree" -p
    "$ours" -p "$theirs")

# Set the branch tip to the new commit
git update-ref "HEAD" "$commit"
```

To use this custom merge strategy, you would save it as a script (let's say custom-ours.sh) and make it executable. Then you would configure Git to use the script as the merge driver for a specific file pattern in your .gitconfig file:

```
[merge "custom-ours"]
name = always choose changes from current branch
driver = /path/to/custom-ours.sh %O %A %B
recursive = binary
```

Here, we've named the merge strategy custom-ours and specified the path to our custom merge script. We've also set the recursive option to binary, which tells Git not to try to merge files that have conflicts.

To use the custom merge strategy for a specific file pattern (e.g. all files with the .txt extension), you would add the following to your .gitattributes file:

```
*.txt merge=custom-ours
```

Now, when you run git merge with changes in a .txt file, Git will use our custom merge script instead of the default recursive strategy. Note that you can also specify the merge strategy explicitly on the command line using the -s option:

```
git merge -s custom-ours <other-branch>
```

Custom merge strategies can be a powerful tool for handling complex merge scenarios in Git, but they should be used with care and tested thoroughly to ensure they behave as expected.

4.16 What is the Git 'replace' command, and what are some use cases for it?

The git replace command is a feature in Git that allows developers to replace an object in the Git object database with another object, such as a commit, tag, or tree. This replacement is not permanent and can be undone at any time.

The git replace command can be useful in a number of scenarios. For example, it can be used to fix mistakes in a commit or a series of commits without having to rewrite history. It can also be used to create a temporary fix while waiting for a proper fix to be implemented. Additionally, git replace can be used to create custom views of the repository, such as a tree that reorganizes the directory structure.

Here is an example of how to use git replace to replace a commit with a new one:

```
$ git replace 123abc new-commit
```

This command replaces the commit with the SHA-1 hash "123abc" with the new commit specified. From this point on, Git treats the replacement commit as if it were the original commit.

To undo the replacement, you can use the –delete option:

```
$ git replace --delete 123abc
```

This command removes the replacement object and restores the original object in the Git object database.

It's worth noting that git replace is a powerful command that should be used with care. In particular, replacing a commit can have unintended consequences if other branches or commits rely on that commit. For this reason, it is generally recommended to avoid using git replace on public repositories or in collaboration with others.

4.17 How do you use 'git worktree' to manage multiple working directories for a single Git repository?

git worktree is a Git command that allows you to manage multiple working directories for a single Git repository. It enables you to work on multiple branches or versions of a project simultaneously, without needing to switch back and forth between different directories or clone the repository multiple times.

Here's how to use git worktree:

1. Create a new worktree

You can create a new worktree using the following command:

```
git worktree add <path>
```

This creates a new worktree at the specified path. By default, the new worktree will be created based on the current branch in the original repository.

For example, to create a new worktree at /path/to/new-worktree:

```
git worktree add /path/to/new-worktree
```

2. Switch between worktrees

You can switch between worktrees using the cd command. Each worktree has its own working directory and .git directory.

For example, to switch to the new worktree created in step 1:

```
cd /path/to/new-worktree
```

3. Remove a worktree

You can remove a worktree using the following command:

```
git worktree remove <path>
```

For example, to remove the worktree at /path/to/new-worktree:

```
git worktree remove /path/to/new-worktree
```

4. List worktrees

You can list all the worktrees associated with a repository using the following command:

```
git worktree list
```

This will show you all the worktrees, along with their paths and the branches they are based on.

5. Customizing worktree settings

You can customize the settings for each worktree by using the --work-tree and --git-dir options with Git commands. For example, to run a git status command in the new worktree:

```
git --work-tree=/path/to/new-worktree --git-dir=/path/to/original-repo/.git
    status
```

This will show the status of the new worktree, rather than the original repository.

In summary, git worktree is a useful command for managing multiple working directories for a single Git repository. It allows you to work on different branches or versions of a project simultaneously, without needing to switch back and forth between different directories or clone the repository multiple times.

4.18 How do you use 'git bundle' to share a repository without using a remote server?

Git bundle is a command-line utility in Git that allows you to create and share a repository without using a remote server. It packages all the necessary Git objects and references into a single file, which can be used to transfer a repository over a network or store it in an archive.

Here's how to create a bundle file:

```
git bundle create repo.bundle HEAD master
```

This command creates a bundle file called repo.bundle that contains all the Git objects and references necessary to represent the current state of the HEAD and master branches.

You can transfer this bundle file to another location using any method you prefer, such as email or USB drive. Once you have the bundle file on another machine, you can extract it into a new Git repository using the git clone command with the –bare and –mirror options:

```
git clone --bare --mirror repo.bundle new-repo.git
```

This creates a new repository called new-repo.git that is an exact copy of the original repository, including all branches, tags, and commits.

Using git bundle has several advantages over other methods of sharing a repository. It allows you to transfer a repository without requiring network access or a remote server, which can be useful in situations where you don't have reliable internet access or when you want to share a repository with someone who doesn't have access to your server. It also provides a secure way to transfer a repository, as the bundle file is signed by the creator's GPG key, ensuring the integrity of the repository contents.

4.19   Can you describe Git's internal mechanisms for handling file renames and moves?

Git has a powerful mechanism for detecting and tracking file renames and moves in a repository's history. This is important because renaming or moving a file in a project is a common operation that developers perform, and it is essential to be able to track such changes in order to understand how the project has evolved over time.

Git uses a heuristic algorithm to detect file renames and moves, based on the content of the files being compared. When you commit changes that rename or move a file, Git calculates a "similarity score" between the old file and the new file. If the score is high enough (default threshold is 50%), Git assumes that the file has been renamed or moved, rather than deleted and a new file added.

Git tracks file renames and moves using a special data structure called the "rename/copy score". This is a table that maps pairs of file paths to a similarity score. When you run git log or other commands that show the history of a repository, Git uses this table to display the correct file names for renamed or moved files, as well as to display information about the history of those files.

For example, let's say you have a file called oldfile.txt in your repository, and you want to rename it to newfile.txt. You can use the git mv command to do this:

```
$ git mv oldfile.txt newfile.txt
```

When you commit this change, Git will automatically detect the rename and track it in the repository's history. If you run git log to view the commit history, you will see that the old file name is displayed with the new file name in parentheses, like this:

```
commit abcdef1234567890abcdef1234567890abcdef12
Author: John Doe <john@example.com>
Date:   Fri Mar 25 16:45:32 2022 -0400

Rename oldfile.txt to newfile.txt

This commit renames the oldfile.txt file to newfile.txt, to better
reflect its contents.

diff --git a/oldfile.txt b/newfile.txt
similarity index 100%
rename from oldfile.txt
rename to newfile.txt
```

The git log output shows that the file was renamed with a 100% similarity score, which means that Git is confident that it is the same file. The old file name is displayed with the new file name in the diff section of the output, and the rename is indicated in the "rename from" and "rename to" lines.

Overall, Git's mechanisms for handling file renames and moves are very robust and powerful. They allow developers to make changes to the organization of their projects while still maintaining a clear and accurate history of the project's evolution over time.

4.20 What are some best practices for managing large-scale Git repositories with multiple teams and projects?

Managing large-scale Git repositories with multiple teams and projects requires careful planning and coordination to ensure efficient collaboration and minimize potential conflicts. Here are some best practices for managing large-scale Git repositories:

Adopt a standardized Git workflow: Adopting a standardized Git workflow across all teams and projects helps to maintain consistency and minimize confusion. Git workflows like Gitflow, GitHub flow, and GitLab flow provide a structured approach to branching, merging, and releasing code.

Use Git submodules or subtrees: Git submodules or subtrees allow you to manage nested repositories within a single repository. This can be useful when you have multiple teams working on separate projects that are interdependent.

Set up code review processes: Code review processes can help ensure code quality and minimize conflicts. Use tools like GitHub or GitLab pull requests to streamline code review processes and provide feedback.

Implement branching strategies: Implementing branching strategies can help minimize conflicts and streamline development processes. Use strategies like feature branching or release branching to isolate code changes and facilitate collaboration.

Use Git hooks: Git hooks are scripts that run automatically before or after specific Git events. Use Git hooks to enforce code formatting, run tests, or perform other custom actions.

Use Git attributes to manage file types: Git attributes allow you to specify custom settings for specific file types, such as ignoring whitespace or setting line endings. This can help maintain consistency across different platforms and development environments.

Use Git tags and releases: Use Git tags and releases to manage versions of your codebase. This can help facilitate communication and collaboration between teams and projects.

Overall, managing large-scale Git repositories requires a combination of standardized processes, effective collaboration tools, and efficient workflows. By implementing best practices and continually iterating on your development processes, you can streamline collaboration and ensure high-quality code.

Chapter 5

Expert

5.1 Can you discuss Git's internal storage mechanism, including the role of loose objects and packfiles?

Git uses a distributed version control system (DVCS) that stores data in a content-addressable database. This database is a collection of Git objects, which include blobs, trees, commits, and tags.

A blob is a binary large object that stores the content of a file. Blobs represent the contents of files, but not their metadata or location in the file system.

A tree is a Git object that represents a directory. It contains references to other trees and blobs, representing the file system structure of a project.

A commit is a Git object that contains a snapshot of the repository at a given point in time, along with metadata such as the author, commit message, and a pointer to the previous commit. Commits are organized in a directed acyclic graph (DAG), with each commit pointing to its parent commit or commits.

A tag is a Git object that allows a developer to assign a symbolic name to a specific version of a repository. It can be used to mark important points in the development history, such as release points.

Git stores these objects as loose objects, which are individual files in the Git object database. When there are many loose objects, Git can pack them into a packfile for more efficient storage and transfer. Packfiles contain multiple objects that are compressed and delta-encoded to reduce their size.

When you clone a Git repository, you receive a complete copy of the object database, including all the loose objects and packfiles. Git uses a SHA-1 hash to identify each object, so it's easy to determine if two repositories have the same content.

In summary, Git's internal storage mechanism is designed to efficiently store and manage large amounts of data in a content-addressable database. By storing objects as loose objects or packfiles, Git can minimize the storage space required and make it easy to share and collaborate on code across multiple repositories.

5.2 How does Git's content-addressable storage work, and how does it contribute to Git's performance?

Git's content-addressable storage is a fundamental aspect of its design and contributes significantly to its performance. Git uses a unique identifier called a SHA-1 hash to identify every object in the repository, including blobs, trees, commits, and tags.

When you create or modify an object in the Git repository, Git calculates the SHA-1 hash of the object's content, and this hash becomes the object's identifier. The content-addressable storage ensures that no two objects in the repository have the same identifier, which guarantees that the repository's content is always consistent and unambiguous.

Git's content-addressable storage contributes to its performance in several ways. First, it enables Git to quickly determine if an object is already present in the repository by checking its hash value. If the object's hash matches an existing object in the repository, Git can reuse that object instead of creating a new one, which reduces the amount of disk space required and speeds up operations.

Second, the content-addressable storage allows Git to perform efficient deduplication of objects. If multiple files in the repository have the same content, Git only needs to store a single copy of the content as a blob object and can reference that object from multiple tree objects. This approach significantly reduces the storage required for large repositories with many similar files.

Finally, Git's content-addressable storage enables efficient cloning and transferring of repositories. Because every object in the repository has a unique identifier based on its content, Git can easily determine which objects are missing from a clone and transfer only those objects. This approach is much more efficient than transferring entire repositories or using binary deltas, which are common in other version control systems.

In summary, Git's content-addressable storage is a critical aspect of its design and enables many of its performance benefits. By using SHA-1 hashes to uniquely identify every object in the repository, Git can efficiently store, deduplicate, and transfer large repositories while maintaining consistency and accuracy.

5.3 How do you recover lost commits or branches in Git using the 'git reflog' and 'git fsck' commands?

In Git, it is possible to recover lost commits or branches using the git reflog and git fsck commands. The git reflog command displays a log of all the references that have been updated in the repository, including the commit history, branch history, and HEAD position. This command is useful for tracking down lost commits or branches that may have been accidentally deleted or overwritten.

Here are the steps to recover lost commits or branches using git reflog and git fsck:

First, use the git reflog command to find the commit or branch that was lost. The output of this command will show the history of all changes to the repository, including branch and HEAD movements.

```
$ git reflog
```

Identify the commit or branch that was lost from the output of the git reflog command, and make a note of its SHA hash or branch name.

Use the git fsck command to check the integrity of the repository's object database. This command will scan the database for any corrupted or missing objects and display a report.

```
$ git fsck --lost-found
```

The git fsck command will generate a list of dangling commits, which are commits that are not connected to any branch or tag. Look for the lost commit or branch in this list.

Once you have identified the lost commit or branch, create a new branch at that commit using the git branch command. For example:

```
$ git branch recover-commit 123abc
```

If you have recovered a branch, switch to that branch using the git checkout command. For example:

```
$ git checkout recover-branch
```

If you have recovered a commit, you can create a new branch from that commit and switch to it using the following commands:

```
$ git branch new-branch 123abc
$ git checkout new-branch
```

By following these steps, you can recover lost commits or branches in Git using the git reflog and git fsck commands. It is important to note that these commands should be used with caution, as they can modify the repository's history and should be used only when necessary.

5.4 Can you explain Git's three-way merge algorithm and its handling of merge conflicts?

Git's three-way merge algorithm is the default algorithm used to combine changes from two different branches or commits. It involves a three-way comparison of the base version (i.e., the common ancestor of the two branches), the source branch (i.e., the branch being merged into the destination branch), and the destination branch (i.e., the branch into which the changes are being merged).

When Git encounters a conflict between the source and destination branches, it tries to automatically merge the changes from both branches by applying the three-way merge algorithm. If Git determines that the changes can be automatically merged without conflicts, it applies the changes and creates a new commit on the destination branch.

However, if Git determines that the changes cannot be automatically merged, it will flag the conflict and pause the merge process, giving the user the opportunity to manually resolve the conflict. Git will mark the conflicted file with conflict markers, indicating the conflicting lines in the file, and will also create backup files that contain the original and modified versions of the conflicting file.

To resolve the conflict, the user must edit the conflicted file, remove the conflict markers, and manually merge the changes from both branches. After resolving the conflict, the user can then add the file to the staging area and continue with the merge process.

Overall, Git's three-way merge algorithm provides a robust and flexible way to merge changes from multiple branches while handling conflicts gracefully.

5.5 How do you design and implement a custom Git workflow tailored to a specific development team's needs?

Designing and implementing a custom Git workflow requires careful consideration of the team's needs and goals, as well as the nature of the project being developed. Here are some key steps to follow:

Identify the team's needs: Start by gathering feedback from team members about their pain points and areas where the current workflow could be improved. Are there specific bottlenecks, such as merge conflicts or code reviews, that are slowing down development? Are there certain features or functionality that the team would like to see incorporated into the workflow? This information will help guide the design of the new workflow.

Define the branching strategy: The branching strategy is a key component of any Git workflow. Consider factors such as the size and complexity of the project, the number of developers on the team, and the frequency of releases when choosing a branching strategy. For example, a simple workflow may use a single main branch and feature branches, while a more complex project may require multiple release branches, hotfix branches, and long-lived branches for ongoing development.

Choose a code review process: Code review is a crucial part of any development workflow, as it ensures that code changes are high-quality, well-tested, and aligned with the project's goals. Determine the code review process that works best for your team. This may include peer review, pull requests, or a combination of both.

Automate as much as possible: Look for opportunities to automate repetitive tasks and reduce the chance of errors. This might include automated testing, continuous integration, and automated code quality checks. The goal is to create a workflow that allows developers to focus on writing code, rather than on manual processes.

Communicate the new workflow: Once the new workflow is defined, communicate it clearly to the team. Provide training and documentation to ensure that everyone is on the same page and understands how the new workflow works.

Here is an example of a custom Git workflow that might work well for a small development team working on a web application:

The team uses a single main branch, called 'master', which is always stable and ready for deployment.

Each developer creates a feature branch for each new feature or bug fix they are working on. These branches are named descriptively, such as 'user-login-feature' or 'shopping-cart-bugfix'.

When a developer has completed work on a feature branch, they create a pull request to merge their changes into the 'master' branch. Other team members review the code changes and provide feedback, which the developer incorporates as needed.

Automated tests are run on the code changes to ensure that they do not introduce any regressions or bugs.

Once the pull request is approved and the tests pass, the changes are merged into the 'master' branch.

The team uses tags to mark each release of the application, so it is easy to track which version of the code is currently in production.

By following these steps, it is possible to create a custom Git workflow that fits the needs of the development team and allows for efficient, high-quality code development.

5.6 How do you configure and manage access control in a Git repository, including using Gitolite or other access management tools?

Git repositories can contain sensitive information that needs to be protected from unauthorized access. Access control allows repository owners to restrict who can view, modify, or delete the contents of a repository. In Git, access control is typically managed using the built-in authentication mechanisms of the underlying file system or server software, or by using third-party access management tools like Gitolite.

Gitolite is a popular open-source access management tool for Git repositories. It allows administrators to set up fine-grained access control rules that can be applied to individual repositories or groups of repositories. Gitolite works by intercepting Git commands sent over SSH, and using a set of configuration files to determine which users are allowed to perform each command.

To configure Gitolite, the administrator must first install it on the server that will host the Git repositories. Once installed, Gitolite provides a web interface for managing access control rules. The administrator can create new repositories, assign permissions to individual users or groups, and set up advanced access control rules based on branch names, file paths, or other criteria.

In addition to Gitolite, other access management tools such as GitHub, GitLab, and Bitbucket also provide access control features. These tools typically offer a web-based interface for managing access control, as well as additional features such as code review, issue tracking, and continuous integration.

When managing access control in Git, it is important to follow best practices to ensure the security and integrity of the repository. These include:

Limiting access to only those who need it Using strong passwords or other authentication mechanisms Regularly reviewing and auditing access logs Encrypting communication between the client and server Keeping the server software and access management tools up to date with the latest security patches.

5.7 What are some strategies for maintaining a healthy Git repository, including periodic maintenance tasks and performance optimizations?

Maintaining a healthy Git repository is essential to ensure the smooth functioning of the repository, and here are some strategies for maintaining a healthy Git repository:

Regularly clean up the repository: It's important to regularly clean up the repository by removing unnecessary files, stale branches, and other objects that are no longer needed. This helps keep the repository clean and fast. You can use the git gc command to perform garbage collection and clean up the repository.

Use Git LFS for large files: Large files can quickly bloat the repository and make it slow. To avoid this, it's recommended to use Git LFS (Large File Storage) to manage large files separately. Git LFS replaces large files with pointers, making the repository smaller and faster.

Use Git submodules or subtrees: When working on a large project that consists of multiple sub-projects, it's recommended to use Git submodules or subtrees to manage the projects separately. This helps keep the repository organized and easy to manage.

Regularly merge changes from upstream: To ensure that the repository is up to date with the latest changes, it's important to regularly merge changes from upstream. This helps avoid conflicts and ensures that the repository is always in sync with the latest changes.

Use Git hooks: Git hooks can be used to automate tasks and enforce standards. For example, you can use pre-commit hooks to ensure that all commits have a proper commit message, or use post-receive hooks to trigger automated builds and deployments.

Use Git aliases: Git aliases can be used to create shortcuts for commonly used commands. This helps reduce typing and makes it easier to use Git. For example, you can create an alias for git status as gs, or create an alias for git log as gl.

Use Git config files: Git config files can be used to configure various aspects of Git, such as the default editor, user name, and email address. This helps ensure consistency across multiple developers and reduces the chances of errors.

Regularly backup the repository: It's important to regularly backup the repository to prevent data loss in case of a hardware failure or other disasters. You can use Git's built-in cloning feature to create a backup of the repository.

These are some of the strategies for maintaining a healthy Git repository. By following these best practices, you can ensure that your Git repository is fast, organized, and easy to manage.

5.8 How do you use 'git bisect run' to automate the process of finding a commit that introduced a bug?

The git bisect command is a powerful tool used for debugging and identifying the commit that introduced a bug in a Git repository. It works by using a binary search algorithm to identify the "bad" commit that introduced the bug.

In some cases, manually testing each commit can be a time-consuming process. This is where git bisect run can come in handy. With this command, you can automate the testing process and have Git automatically check out each commit and run a script to determine whether it is "good" or "bad".

Here's an example of how to use git bisect run:

Start by running git bisect start to begin the bisect process. Identify a "bad" commit in your repository by running git bisect bad while on a known bad commit. Identify a "good" commit in your repository by running git bisect good while on a known good commit. Git will automatically check out a commit and prompt you to test it. Instead of manually testing, run a script to automatically determine if the commit is "good" or "bad". You can do this by running git bisect run <test-script> where <test-script> is the path to the script you want to run. Git will start checking out commits and running your test script until it identifies the commit that introduced the bug.

Here's an example test script that you might use with git bisect run:

```
#!/bin/bash

# Build the codebase
make

# Run the test suite
make test

# Check the test results
if grep -q "error" test.log; then
# The commit is bad
exit 1
else
# The commit is good
exit 0
fi
```

In this example, the script first builds the codebase and then runs the test suite. If any errors are found in the test log, the script exits with a status of 1 (indicating a bad commit). If there are no errors, the script exits with a status of 0 (indicating a good commit).

Using git bisect run can save a lot of time and effort when trying to identify the commit that introduced a bug. However, it's important to make sure that your test script is reliable and can accurately determine whether a commit is "good" or "bad".

5.9 Can you discuss some advanced techniques for dealing with large binary files in a Git repository?

Git is a powerful tool for version control, but it is not always well-suited for managing large binary files such as images, audio, video, or compiled binaries. Large binary files can quickly bloat a Git repository, making it difficult to manage, clone, and share. Here are some advanced techniques for dealing with large binary files in Git:

Git Large File Storage (LFS): Git LFS is an open-source extension to Git that allows you to store large binary files outside of the main Git repository, while still tracking them in Git. Git LFS replaces large files with "pointer" files that reference the actual binary files stored in a remote server or cloud service, such as GitHub, Bitbucket, or Amazon S3. This reduces the size of the Git repository and speeds up Git operations, such as cloning and pulling. To use Git LFS, you need to install the Git LFS client and configure your Git repository to use Git LFS.

Git Annex: Git Annex is another open-source extension to Git that allows you to store large binary files outside of the main Git repository. Git Annex uses a content-addressable storage system, similar to Git, to track the location and status of binary files. Git Annex provides various commands to manage binary files, such as adding, removing, copying, and syncing files between repositories. Git Annex can work with local or remote storage, such as external hard drives, cloud services, or peer-to-peer networks.

Git BFG: Git BFG (Big Fast Garbage) is a command-line tool that helps you remove large binary files or other unwanted data from a Git repository. Git BFG is faster and more efficient than Git's native garbage collection mechanism, especially for large repositories. Git BFG can remove files that exceed a certain size, match a certain pattern, or contain certain strings. Git BFG also provides an interactive mode that allows you to review and confirm the changes before applying them.

Git Filter-Repo: Git Filter-Repo is another command-line tool that allows you to rewrite the history of a Git repository by filtering out unwanted files, directories, or commits. Git Filter-Repo is more flexible and powerful than Git BFG, but also more complex to use. Git Filter-Repo provides various filters and options to match and modify the history of a repository, such as –path, –tree-filter, –commit-filter, –env-filter, and –force.

Git Submodules: Git Submodules is a built-in feature of Git that allows you to include one Git repository as a subdirectory of another Git repository. Git Submodules can be used to manage large binary files that are shared across multiple repositories, such as libraries, frameworks, or assets. Git Submodules allow you to reference a specific version of a repository and update it independently from the main repository. However, Git Submodules can also be complex to manage and cause merge conflicts if not used carefully.

Overall, dealing with large binary files in Git requires a combination of tools, techniques, and best practices, depending on the specific needs and constraints of your project. It is important to balance the trade-offs between performance, storage, versioning, and collaboration when choosing a strategy for managing large binary files in Git.

5.10 How do you use 'git rerere' to handle repeated merge conflicts in long-lived branches?

git rerere is a Git command that stands for "reuse recorded resolution". It allows Git to remember how merge conflicts were resolved in the past and apply those resolutions automatically in the future when it encounters similar conflicts.

When two or more branches are merged in Git, conflicts can arise when the same code has been modified in different ways in each branch. Resolving these conflicts can be time-consuming and error-prone, especially when dealing with long-lived branches that are frequently merged.

To use git rerere, you first need to enable it by running the command:

```
$ git config --global rerere.enabled true
```

Once enabled, git rerere will automatically start recording conflict resolutions when you resolve merge conflicts manually. You can then use the recorded resolutions to automatically resolve conflicts in the future by running the command:

```
$ git rerere
```

This command will scan the current repository for recorded resolutions and apply them to any conflicts it encounters.

You can also use the git rerere command to manually resolve merge conflicts using previously recorded resolutions. For example, to resolve a conflict using a previously recorded resolution, you can run:

```
$ git rerere
$ git add <conflicted-file>
$ git commit
```

The git rerere command can save a significant amount of time and effort when dealing with repeated merge conflicts. However, it's important to note that it can also introduce risks if not used carefully. In particular, it's possible for git rerere to apply incorrect resolutions to conflicts, leading to incorrect code changes. Therefore, it's important to review the changes introduced by git rerere carefully and test them thoroughly before committing them to the repository.

5.11 How do you perform advanced Git history rewriting, such as reordering commits, changing commit messages, or modifying the authorship of a commit?

Git is a powerful tool for version control and collaboration, but sometimes you may need to make changes to the commit history. Git history rewriting is a technique that allows you to modify the commit history, including reordering commits, changing commit messages, or modifying the authorship of a commit. However, it's important to use these tools with caution and to communicate with your team if you're working on a shared repository.

Here are some ways to perform advanced Git history rewriting:

Reordering commits: Reordering commits is useful if you want to rearrange the order of changes, such as if you need to revert a change that was made earlier in the history. To reorder commits, you can use Git's interactive rebase feature. This allows you to open an editor to modify the commits in a branch. For example, to reorder the last three commits in a branch, you can use the following command:

```
git rebase -i HEAD~3
```

This will open an editor with the last three commits listed in reverse order. You can modify the order by moving the lines in the editor. For example, to swap the first two commits, you can move the second commit line above the first commit line. Once you've made your changes, you can save the file and exit the editor. Git will then apply the changes and create a new commit history.

Changing commit messages: Changing commit messages is useful if you need to fix a typo or clarify the purpose of a change. To change the commit message of the last commit, you can use the –amend option with the git commit command:

```
git commit --amend -m "New commit message"
```

This will open an editor where you can modify the commit message. Once you've made your changes, you can save the file and exit the editor. Git will then apply the changes and create a new commit history.

Modifying the authorship of a commit: Modifying the authorship of a commit is useful if you need to change the attribution of a change, such as if you made a change on behalf of someone else. To modify the authorship of the last commit, you can use the –reset-author option with the –amend option:

```
git commit --amend --reset-author
```

This will update the author and committer information to match the current user.

It's important to note that Git history rewriting can be a complex and potentially dangerous operation, especially when done on a shared repository. It's important to communicate with your team and agree on a strategy for managing the commit history. It's also a good practice to make a backup or a clone of the repository before performing any advanced history rewriting operations, so you can easily revert back to a previous state if something goes wrong.

In summary, Git history rewriting can be a powerful tool for managing your commit history, but it should be used with care and only when necessary. Reordering commits, changing commit messages, and modifying the authorship of a commit are all possible using Git's built-in features, and understanding how to use them effectively can help you manage your Git history more effectively.

5.12 How do you deal with Git submodules when merging, rebasing, or bisecting?

Git submodules are a powerful feature of Git that allow you to include one Git repository inside another. Submodules can be tricky to work with when merging, rebasing, or bisecting, because they have their own commit history and may have different versions than the parent repository.

Here are some ways to deal with Git submodules when merging, rebasing, or bisecting:

Merging with submodules: When merging a branch that includes a submodule, Git will only merge the submodule reference, not the contents of the submodule. This means that if you want to update the submodule to the latest version, you need to run git submodule update after the merge. For example, if you're merging the feature-branch into the master branch, you can use the following commands:

```
git merge feature-branch
git submodule update
```

This will merge the changes from the feature-branch into the master branch and update the submodule to the latest version.

Rebasing with submodules: Rebasing a branch that includes a submodule can be more complicated, because Git will try to reapply the submodule changes on top of the new base. This can cause conflicts if the submodule has changed in the meantime. To avoid conflicts, you can use the –rebase-merges option with the git rebase command. For example, if you're rebasing the feature-branch onto the master branch, you can use the following command:

```
git rebase --rebase-merges master feature-branch
```

This will perform a merge-style rebase, which will preserve the submodule changes and apply them on top of the new base.

Bisecting with submodules: Bisecting a repository that includes a submodule can also be tricky, because the submodule may have different versions at different points in the commit history. To bisect a repository with submodules, you need to use the –recurse-submodules option with the git bisect command. For example, if you're bisecting the master branch to find a bug, you can use the following command:

```
git bisect start --recurse-submodules master HEAD
```

This will perform the bisect operation recursively on the submodule as well as the parent repository.

It's important to note that Git submodules can be complex and may require additional steps to manage. For example, you may need to clone the submodule separately or update it to a specific version. Additionally, if you're working with a large number of submodules, it may be more efficient to use Git's submodule foreach command to perform operations on all submodules at once.

In summary, dealing with Git submodules when merging, rebasing, or bisecting requires additional care and attention to detail. By understanding the specific requirements of submodules and using Git's built-in commands effectively, you can manage submodules more effectively and avoid potential conflicts or issues in your repository.

5.13 What are the security implications of Git's SHA-1 hashing algorithm, and how does the transition to SHA-256 affect Git workflows?

Git uses SHA-1 hashing algorithm to generate the unique identifiers (hashes) for commits, files, and objects in the repository. SHA-1 is a cryptographic hash function that generates a 160-bit hash value, which is considered to be collision-resistant. However, there are some security implications of using SHA-1, and Git is in the process of transitioning to a more secure hashing algorithm, SHA-256.

Here are the security implications of Git's SHA-1 hashing algorithm:

Collision attacks: While SHA-1 is considered to be collision-resistant, it is not completely immune to collision attacks. In 2017, researchers demonstrated a practical collision attack on SHA-1, which could be used to create two different files with the same hash value. This means that an attacker could potentially create a malicious file that has the same hash value as a legitimate file, and Git would not be able to distinguish between them.

Malicious commits: In Git, a commit hash identifies a particular state of the repository at a given point in time. If an attacker can create a commit with the same hash as a legitimate commit, they can potentially inject malicious code into the repository. While this is difficult to do in practice, it is not impossible, especially if the repository has weak access controls.

Rogue Git servers: When you clone a Git repository, you trust the integrity of the objects and commits in the repository. However, if an attacker can compromise the Git server, they can potentially modify the objects and commits in the repository, and serve them to unsuspecting users. This can be especially dangerous if the repository contains sensitive or confidential information.

To mitigate these security implications, Git is in the process of transitioning to a more secure hashing algorithm, SHA-256. SHA-256 is a more secure hashing algorithm that generates a 256-bit hash value, which is considered to be collision-resistant. This means that the chances of a collision attack are much lower than with SHA-1.

The transition to SHA-256 affects Git workflows in several ways:

Git client support: Git clients need to be updated to support SHA-256 hashing. This means that older Git clients may not be able to clone or work with repositories that use SHA-256.

Git server support: Git servers need to be updated to support SHA-256 hashing. This means that Git hosting providers need to update their infrastructure to support SHA-256.

Repository migration: Repositories that use SHA-1 need to be migrated to SHA-256. This can be a complex process, especially if the repository has a large number of objects or if there are dependencies on legacy Git clients.

In summary, Git's SHA-1 hashing algorithm has some security implications, and Git is transitioning to the more secure SHA-256 hashing algorithm. While this transition may require some updates to Git clients and servers, it will provide greater security for Git repositories and help mitigate the risk of collision attacks and other security threats.

5.14   How do you set up and manage a Git server, such as GitLab or GitHub Enterprise, to meet the needs of a large organization?

Setting up and managing a Git server for a large organization can be a complex process that requires careful planning and implementation. GitLab and GitHub Enterprise are two popular solutions for hosting Git repositories, and both offer a wide range of features and capabilities to meet the needs of a large organization. Here are some steps to set up and manage a Git server for a large organization:

Plan your infrastructure: Before setting up a Git server, you need to plan your infrastructure. This includes deciding on the number of servers, storage requirements, backup and disaster recovery procedures, and access controls. You should also consider the number of users and repositories, as this will affect the performance and scalability of the Git server.

Install and configure the Git server: Once you've planned your infrastructure, you can install and configure the Git server. This includes installing the server software, configuring security settings, and setting up repositories and users. For GitLab and GitHub Enterprise, the installation and configuration process is well-documented and includes a web-based interface for managing users, repositories, and permissions.

Configure access controls: Access controls are critical for ensuring the security of the Git server. This includes setting up user authentication and authorization, implementing two-factor authentication, and configuring SSH keys. You should also consider implementing access controls at the repository level, such as read-only access for certain repositories or restricting access to certain branches.

Implement backup and disaster recovery procedures: Backing up Git repositories is important for ensuring the continuity of the development process in the event of a disaster. This includes implementing automated backups, storing backups offsite, and regularly testing the backup and recovery procedures.

Monitor and optimize performance: Monitoring and optimizing the performance of the Git server is important for ensuring the efficiency of the development process. This includes monitoring server usage, optimizing server configuration, and implementing caching strategies. You should also consider using load balancers and other techniques to distribute the load across multiple servers.

Train and support users: Finally, it's important to train and support users to ensure that they can effectively use the Git server. This includes providing training on Git workflows, best practices for collaboration, and troubleshooting techniques. You should also provide a support mechanism, such as a help desk or online forums, to address any issues that users may encounter.

In summary, setting up and managing a Git server for a large organization requires careful planning and implementation. By following these steps and utilizing the features and capabilities of GitLab and GitHub Enterprise, you can create a secure, scalable, and efficient Git server that meets the needs of your organization.

5.15   What are some advanced techniques for managing Git hooks, including sharing hooks across a team or organization?

Git hooks are scripts that Git runs before or after certain events, such as a commit, a push, or a merge. Git hooks can be used to enforce code standards, perform code analysis, or run tests before changes are committed. Advanced techniques for managing Git hooks can include sharing hooks across a team or organization, setting up hook templates, and using pre-commit hooks to prevent bad commits.

Here are some techniques for managing Git hooks:

Sharing hooks across a team or organization: If you have a team or organization that uses the same hooks, you can share the hooks by placing them in a shared location, such as a shared Git repository or a network drive. Each member of the team can then symlink to the shared hooks. For example, if you have a shared repository named shared-hooks, you can symlink to the pre-commit hook by running the following command:

```
ln -s /path/to/shared-hooks/pre-commit .git/hooks/pre-commit
```

This will create a symlink to the shared pre-commit hook in your local repository.

Setting up hook templates: Git allows you to set up hook templates, which are templates for new repositories that include pre-configured hooks. To set up a hook template, you can create a directory called .git-templates/hooks in your home directory, and then create hooks in that directory. For example, if you want to include a pre-commit hook in the template, you can create a file called .git-templates/hooks/pre-commit with the desired script. Then, you can run the following command to enable the template:

```
git config --global init.templatedir '~/.git-templates'
```

This will set up the template directory, and any new repositories that you create will include the hooks from the template.

Using pre-commit hooks to prevent bad commits: Pre-commit hooks can be used to prevent bad commits, such as commits that don't conform to code standards or that contain security vulnerabilities. For example, you can use a pre-commit hook to run a linter or static code analysis tool before committing changes. If the analysis tool detects any errors, the commit will be rejected. You can also use a pre-commit hook to check for sensitive data, such as API keys or passwords, before committing changes.

Using server-side hooks for additional validation: Git also supports server-side hooks that can be used to enforce additional validation on the server. For example, you can use a server-side hook to enforce access controls, perform security checks, or enforce code review policies. Server-side hooks are stored in the hooks directory of the server-side repository, and are executed on the server before and after specific Git operations.

In summary, managing Git hooks can be an important part of a team or organization's workflow. Advanced techniques for managing Git hooks can include sharing hooks across a team or organization, setting up hook templates, using pre-commit hooks to prevent bad commits, and using server-side hooks for additional validation. By using these techniques, you can enforce code standards, improve code quality, and ensure the security of your codebase.

5.16 Can you explain the concept of "grafts" in Git and provide some use cases for them?

In Git, a "graft" is a way to manually specify parent-child relationships between commits. This can be useful in situations where the repository history needs to be modified, for example, to combine two separate repositories into one or to correct mistakes in the commit history.

Here's how grafts work:

When Git generates the commit graph for a repository, it uses the parent-child relationships between commits to build the graph. Normally, these relationships are determined automatically based on the order of commits in the repository. However, with grafts, you can manually specify parent-child relationships between commits.

To create a graft, you create a file named .git/info/grafts in the repository, and add lines to the file specifying the parent-child relationships between commits. Each line in the file specifies a parent commit and a child commit, separated by a space. For example:

```
<new-parent-commit> <old-child-commit>
```

This tells Git that the <new-parent-commit> should be the parent of the <old-child-commit>. When Git generates the commit graph, it will use these relationships to build the graph.

Here are some use cases for grafts:

Combining repositories: If you have two separate Git repositories that you want to combine into one, you can use grafts to specify the parent-child relationships between the two repositories. This allows Git to generate a single commit graph that includes the history of both repositories.

For example, suppose you have two repositories: repo1.git and repo2.git. You want to combine them into a single repository combined.git. You can do this by creating a graft that specifies the parent-child relationship between the final commit of repo1.git and the first commit of repo2.git. This allows Git to generate a single commit graph that includes the history of both repositories.

Correcting mistakes in the commit history: If you discover a mistake in the commit history, such as a commit that was accidentally attributed to the wrong author, you can use grafts to correct the mistake. By specifying the correct parent-child relationships between the commits, you can modify the commit history without having to rewrite the entire repository.

For example, suppose you have a commit in the repository that was accidentally attributed to the wrong author. You can correct this by creating a graft that specifies the correct parent-child relationship between the commit and its parent. This allows Git to generate a new commit graph that reflects the corrected history.

Reordering commits: If you want to reorder commits in the repository, you can use grafts to specify the new parent-child relationships between the commits. This allows Git to generate a new commit graph that reflects the reordered history.

For example, suppose you have a series of commits in the repository that you want to reorder. You can do this by creating a graft that specifies the new parent-child relationships between the commits. This allows Git to generate a new commit graph that reflects the reordered history.

Converting repositories from other version control systems: If you are converting a repository from another version control system, such as Subversion, to Git, you can use grafts to specify the parent-child relationships between the commits in the new Git repository. This allows Git to generate a commit graph that reflects the history of the original repository.

In summary, grafts are a way to manually specify parent-child relationships between commits in Git. They can be useful in situations where the repository history needs to be modified, such as combining repositories or correcting mistakes in the commit history. By using grafts, you can modify the commit history without having to rewrite the entire repository.

5.17 How do you implement continuous integration and deployment workflows using Git?

Continuous Integration (CI) and Continuous Deployment (CD) are essential components of modern software development workflows, enabling teams to quickly and efficiently build, test, and deploy code changes. Git is a powerful tool that can be used to implement CI/CD workflows, providing teams with the ability to automate the build, test, and deployment process.

Here are some steps for implementing CI/CD workflows using Git:

Set up a version control system: The first step in implementing a CI/CD workflow using Git is to set up a version control system. This can be done using a hosted service such as GitHub, GitLab, or Bitbucket, or by setting up a Git server in-house.

Create a development branch: Once the version control system is set up, the next step is to create a development branch. This branch will be used for ongoing development work and will serve as the basis for all future feature branches.

Create feature branches: With the development branch in place, individual developers can create feature branches to work on specific features or bug fixes. Each feature branch should be created from the development branch, and changes should be made and tested on the feature branch before being merged back into the development branch.

Implement automated testing: In order to ensure that code changes are properly tested, automated testing should be implemented. This can be done using a variety of tools, such as Travis CI or Jenkins, and can include unit tests, integration tests, and acceptance tests.

Use pull requests for code reviews: Before changes are merged back into the development branch, they should be reviewed by other team members. This can be done using pull requests, which provide a way for team members to review code changes and suggest modifications before they are merged.

Implement continuous deployment: Once changes have been tested and reviewed, they can be merged back into the development branch and deployed to the production environment. This can be done using a variety of tools, such as GitLab CI/CD or Jenkins, and can include steps such as building the application, testing the application, and deploying the application to production.

Here's an example workflow for implementing CI/CD using Git:

A developer creates a new feature branch from the development branch.

The developer makes changes to the code and tests the changes locally.

The developer creates a pull request, which triggers automated testing using a tool such as Travis CI.

Other team members review the pull request and suggest modifications if necessary.

Once the pull request is approved, the changes are merged into the development branch.

Automated deployment is triggered, which builds and deploys the application to the production environment.

In summary, Git can be used to implement powerful CI/CD workflows, providing teams with the ability to automate the build, test, and deployment process. By using Git to manage code changes and integrating it with automated testing and deployment tools, teams can quickly and efficiently deploy changes to the production environment.

5.18 What are some strategies for using Git with other version control systems, such as SVN or Mercurial, in a mixed environment?

When working in a mixed version control environment, where different teams or systems use different version control systems (VCS), it can be challenging to maintain consistency and collaboration across the various systems. Git provides tools to integrate with other VCSs, such as SVN or Mercurial, allowing teams to work together more efficiently. Here are some strategies for using Git with other VCSs in a mixed environment:

Use Git-SVN or Git-Hg: Git provides two built-in tools, Git-SVN and Git-Hg, for interacting with SVN and Mercurial repositories, respectively. These tools allow you to use Git to manage changes in a repository that is otherwise managed by SVN or Mercurial. This can be particularly useful if you are working in a team that uses SVN or Mercurial, but you prefer to use Git for your own development work.

Use SubGit or Hg-Git: SubGit and Hg-Git are two third-party tools that allow you to integrate Git with SVN or Mercurial repositories, respectively. These tools provide more comprehensive integration than Git-SVN or Git-Hg, allowing you to use Git for all development work while still synchronizing with the SVN or Mercurial repository. This can be particularly useful if you are part of a team that uses both Git and SVN or Mercurial, and you want to maintain a single codebase across both systems.

Use a Git-SVN Bridge or Git-Hg Bridge: A Git-SVN bridge or Git-Hg bridge provides a way to automatically synchronize changes between a Git repository and an SVN or Mercurial repository. This allows teams to work in their preferred VCS, while still collaborating across multiple systems. These bridges can be particularly useful for larger teams or projects where multiple VCSs are in use.

Use Git as a centralized repository: If your team is working in a mixed environment and needs to maintain a single codebase across multiple VCSs, you can use Git as a centralized repository. Each team member can use their preferred VCS for local development work, and changes can be pushed to a centralized Git repository, where they can be merged and synchronized across all VCSs. This can be particularly useful for larger projects where multiple teams or systems are involved.

In summary, Git provides a range of tools and strategies for integrating with other VCSs in a mixed environment. By using tools such as Git-SVN, Git-Hg, SubGit, Hg-Git, Git-SVN bridges, Git-Hg bridges, or Git as a centralized repository, teams can work in their preferred VCS while still collaborating across multiple systems.

5.19 How do you use 'git subtree' to manage large projects with multiple components and their dependencies?

When working on a large project with multiple components and their dependencies, it can be challenging to manage changes and dependencies across the various components. Git provides a built-in tool, git subtree, that can help with managing these dependencies and changes across different parts of a project. Here's how to use git subtree:

Adding a Subtree: To add a subtree to your project, use the following command:

```
git subtree add --prefix=<prefix> <repository> <branch> --squash
```

This command adds the remote repository as a subtree of your project, and checks out the specified branch. The –prefix option specifies the path where the subtree will be added within your project, and the –squash option ensures that only a single commit is created for the subtree changes.

For example, to add the components/foo directory of the myproject repository as a subtree of your project:

```
git subtree add --prefix=components/foo https://github.com/myproject.git
     master --squash
```

Updating a Subtree: To update a subtree, use the following command:

```
git subtree pull --prefix=<prefix> <repository> <branch> --squash
```

This command pulls changes from the remote repository and merges them into the specified subtree within your project. The –prefix option specifies the path of the subtree, and the –squash option ensures that only a single commit is created for the subtree changes.

For example, to update the components/foo subtree from the myproject repository:

```
git subtree pull --prefix=components/foo https://github.com/myproject.git
     master --squash
```

Pushing Changes to a Subtree: To push changes to a subtree, use the following command:

```
git subtree push --prefix=<prefix> <repository> <branch>
```

This command pushes changes from the specified subtree to the remote repository. The –prefix option specifies the path of the subtree, and the –branch option specifies the branch to push changes to.

For example, to push changes from the components/foo subtree to the myproject repository:

```
git subtree push --prefix=components/foo https://github.com/myproject.git
     master
```

Removing a Subtree: To remove a subtree, use the following command:

```
git subtree remove --prefix=<prefix> <repository> <branch>
```

This command removes the subtree from your project and the specified remote repository. The –prefix option specifies the path of the subtree, and the –branch option specifies the branch to remove.

For example, to remove the components/foo subtree from the myproject repository:

```
git subtree remove --prefix=components/foo https://github.com/myproject.git
    master
```

Using git subtree can make it easier to manage large projects with multiple components and their dependencies. By adding, updating, and pushing changes to subtrees, you can maintain a modular and organized project structure while still being able to collaborate and manage dependencies across different components.

5.20 Can you discuss the limitations of Git's distributed model and propose solutions for dealing with issues like repository size, performance, and collaboration in large teams?

Git's distributed model provides many benefits, such as easy branching and merging, offline work, and decentralized collaboration. However, it also has some limitations, especially when working with large repositories and large teams. Here are some of the limitations of Git's distributed model and some solutions for dealing with these issues:

Repository Size: Git's distributed model is not well-suited for managing very large repositories with many binary files or other large files. This is because every copy of the repository must contain a complete copy of all files and their history, which can result in very large repositories that are slow to clone and consume a lot of disk space.

Solution: To deal with large repositories, you can use Git's git-lfs (Large File Storage) extension, which allows you to store large files outside of your Git repository and only download them as needed. You can also consider splitting your repository into smaller, more manageable repositories that focus on specific areas of your project.

Performance: Git's distributed model can suffer from performance issues, especially when dealing with large repositories or performing complex operations like merging.

Solution: To improve performance, you can use Git's git-repack command to pack objects in your repository more efficiently, which can reduce the size of your repository and improve performance. You can also use git-gc to remove unnecessary objects and optimize the repository. Additionally, using Git's –depth option when cloning repositories can reduce the amount of data downloaded and speed up the process.

Collaboration in Large Teams: Git's distributed model can make collaboration in large teams more difficult, especially when many people are working on the same files or branches.

Solution: To deal with collaboration issues, you can use Git's git-merge and git-rebase commands to manage changes and merge them into the main branch. You can also use Git's pull request feature to review and merge changes made by other team members. Additionally, using a centralized repository, such as GitLab or GitHub, can help manage collaboration and provide tools for code review and management.

Security: Git's distributed model can create security concerns when many people have access to the repository and its history.

Solution: To deal with security concerns, you can use Git's access controls and authentication features to control who has access to the repository and what they can do with it. You can also use Git's git-verify-commit command to verify the integrity of commits and ensure that they have not been tampered with.

In summary, while Git's distributed model provides many benefits, it also has some limitations when dealing with large repositories and teams. To deal with these issues, you can use Git's git-lfs extension, git-repack and git-gc commands to manage repository size and performance, use git-merge, git-rebase, and pull requests to manage collaboration, and use access controls and authentication to manage security concerns.

Chapter 6

Guru

6.1 How do you handle repositories with extremely large files, and what are the performance implications of such repositories in Git?

Git is designed to handle most types of files, but it can become difficult to work with extremely large files. Large files can slow down Git operations, take up a lot of disk space, and make repositories difficult to manage. In this answer, we will discuss how to handle repositories with extremely large files and the performance implications of such repositories in Git.

Handling Repositories with Large Files Git Large File Storage (LFS)

Git Large File Storage (LFS) is an open-source Git extension that manages large files separately from the Git repository. Instead of storing large files in the Git repository, LFS stores them on a server and replaces them in the Git repository with pointers that refer to the actual file. This can significantly reduce the size of the Git repository and improve performance.

To use Git LFS, you need to install the LFS command-line tool and enable it in your Git repository. You can then specify which files should be managed by LFS using Git attributes.

Git Annex

Git Annex is another open-source Git extension that manages large files separately from the Git repository. Git Annex stores large files in a separate repository, and replaces them in the Git repository with symbolic links. This can also significantly reduce the size of the Git repository and improve performance.

To use Git Annex, you need to install the Git Annex command-line tool and enable it in your Git repository. You can then specify which files should be managed by Git Annex using Git attributes.

Git Submodules

Git submodules allow you to include a separate Git repository within your main repository as a subdirectory. This can be useful for managing large files that are associated with a specific part of your codebase.

To use Git submodules, you can add the submodule using the git submodule add command. This will create a separate repository in the specified subdirectory. You can then commit the changes to your main repository, which will include the submodule as a pointer to the specific commit in the submodule repository.

Performance Implications

Working with extremely large files in Git can have significant performance implications. Some of the issues that can arise include:

Slow performance when cloning or fetching large repositories Increased disk usage due to the size of large files Slow performance when diffing or merging large files Difficulty in managing large files in Git

Using Git LFS, Git Annex, or Git submodules can help mitigate some of these issues by separating large files from the Git repository. However, it is still important to be aware of the performance implications of large files in Git and to design your Git workflow accordingly.

In summary, handling repositories with extremely large files in Git can be challenging. Using Git LFS, Git Annex, or Git submodules can help manage large files and improve performance. However, it is important to be aware of the performance implications of large files in Git and design your Git workflow accordingly.

6.2 Can you discuss the trade-offs between using a monorepo versus a multi-repo setup in a large organization?

When managing a large organization's codebase, one important decision to make is whether to use a monorepo or a multi-repo setup. Both approaches have their advantages and disadvantages, and the choice depends on the organization's specific needs and priorities.

Monorepo

A monorepo is a single, centralized repository that contains all the code for an organization's software projects. Some advantages of using a monorepo include:

Easier cross-project changes: With all code in one place, it is easier to make changes that span multiple projects. This can be particularly useful for shared libraries or code that is reused across projects. Better code visibility: With a monorepo, it is easier to see all the code for an organization's projects in one place, which can improve code understanding and help with maintenance. Simplified build and deployment: A monorepo can make it easier to manage build and deployment processes across multiple projects, as there is only one repository to work with.

However, there are also some potential drawbacks to using a monorepo, including:

Complexity: A monorepo can become very large and complex, which can make it difficult to manage and navigate. Risk of code coupling: With all code in one repository, there is a risk that changes in one area of the code can have unintended effects on other areas of the code. Increased risk of merge conflicts: With all code in one repository, there is a higher likelihood of merge conflicts, particularly when multiple teams are working on different parts of the codebase. Multi-Repo

A multi-repo setup involves using separate repositories for each project or component of an organization's codebase. Some advantages of using a multi-repo setup include:

Easier management of independent projects: With each project in a separate repository, it is easier to manage code changes and dependencies within each project independently. Less complexity: Multi-repo setups can be less complex than monorepos, which can make it easier to manage and navigate. Reduced risk of merge conflicts: With separate repositories for each project, there is a lower likelihood of merge conflicts, as changes in one repository are less likely to affect other repositories.

However, there are also some potential drawbacks to using a multi-repo setup, including:

Difficulty with cross-project changes: With each project in a separate repository, it can be more difficult to make changes that span multiple projects, particularly if there are complex dependencies between projects. Reduced code visibility: With each project in a separate repository, it can be more difficult to see all the code for an organization's projects in one place, which can make maintenance and code understanding more difficult. More complex build and deployment processes: With separate repositories for each project, it can be more complex to manage build and deployment processes across multiple projects.

In summary, both monorepos and multi-repo setups have their advantages and disadvantages. Monorepos can be useful for organizations that have a lot of shared code and need to make changes that span multiple projects. However, they can also be more complex and have a higher risk of merge conflicts. Multi-repo setups can be useful for organizations that need to manage independent projects, but they can be more difficult to manage and may require more complex build and deployment processes. The choice between a monorepo and a multi-repo setup depends on the specific needs and priorities of the organization.

6.3 What are some advanced Git branching models and best practices for managing complex projects with multiple releases and parallel development?

Git provides a powerful branching and merging model that can be used to manage complex projects with multiple releases and parallel development. In this answer, we will discuss some advanced Git branching models and best practices for managing complex projects.

Gitflow

Gitflow is a popular branching model that provides a set of guidelines for managing Git branches in a structured manner. The Gitflow model defines two main branches: master and develop. The master branch contains production-ready code, while the develop branch contains the latest code that is being actively developed.

In addition to the master and develop branches, Gitflow also defines several types of feature branches, release branches, and hotfix branches. Feature branches are used for developing new features, release branches are used for preparing for a new release, and hotfix branches are used for fixing critical bugs in production code.

Gitflow provides a clear structure for managing Git branches and can be particularly useful for teams that have well-defined release cycles and want to ensure that production code is always stable.

Trunk-based Development

Trunk-based development is a branching model that encourages developers to work on a single codebase, with all changes made directly to the master branch. Instead of creating feature branches, developers make changes directly to the master branch and use feature flags or other techniques to ensure that changes are not immediately visible to end-users.

Trunk-based development can be useful for teams that want to move quickly and iterate rapidly. However, it can also require careful management to ensure that code quality remains high and that changes do not negatively impact other parts of the codebase.

Best Practices for Managing Git Branches

Regardless of the branching model used, there are several best practices for managing Git branches in a complex project:

Keep branches small and focused: Branches should be small and focused on specific features or bug fixes. This can make it easier to manage branches and reduce the risk of merge conflicts. Use feature flags: Feature flags can be used to control the visibility of new features, allowing them to be gradually rolled out to users and reducing the risk of breaking changes. Regularly merge changes: Changes should be regularly merged back into the main branch to ensure that the codebase remains up-to-date and that there are no surprises when it comes time to release. Use pull requests: Pull requests can be used to review code changes and ensure that they meet quality standards before being merged into the main branch. Automate tests and builds: Automated tests and builds can help ensure that code changes do not introduce new bugs or break existing functionality.

In summary, Git provides a powerful branching and merging model that can be used to manage complex projects with multiple releases and parallel development. The Gitflow and trunk-based development models are two popular approaches for managing Git branches. Regardless of the model used, best practices such as keeping branches small and focused, using feature flags, regularly merging changes, using pull requests, and automating tests and builds can help ensure that the codebase remains stable and high-quality.

6.4 How do you set up and manage Git LFS (Large File Storage) at scale for a large organization?

Git LFS (Large File Storage) is a Git extension that allows large files to be managed in Git repositories more efficiently. Setting up and managing Git LFS at scale for a large organization can be a complex process, but with the right approach, it can be done effectively.

Setting up Git LFS

To set up Git LFS, you will need to follow these steps:

Install Git LFS on all developer machines: Git LFS must be installed on all developer machines to enable large file management.

Configure Git LFS on the Git server: Git LFS must be configured on the Git server to allow large files to be stored and retrieved.

Configure the Git client: The Git client must be configured to use Git LFS.

Managing Git LFS at Scale

Once Git LFS has been set up, managing it at scale for a large organization involves several best practices:

Define a LFS policy: Define a LFS policy that outlines what types of files should be managed by LFS and what size limit should be set.

Use LFS pointers: LFS pointers can be used to replace large files in Git with small pointers. This can help reduce the size of the repository and speed up cloning and pulling.

Use LFS hooks: LFS hooks can be used to enforce the LFS policy, automatically convert large files to LFS pointers, and reject commits that violate the policy.

Monitor LFS usage: Monitor LFS usage to ensure that the LFS policy is being followed and to identify any potential issues with LFS usage.

Back up LFS objects: Back up LFS objects to ensure that large files can be restored in the event of data loss.

Use LFS filters: LFS filters can be used to automatically convert large files to LFS pointers during Git operations, such as cloning and pulling.

Manage LFS access: Manage LFS access to ensure that only authorized users have access to large files.

Example Workflow

Here is an example workflow for using Git LFS at scale for a large organization:

Define a LFS policy that outlines what types of files should be managed by LFS and what size limit should be set.

Install and configure Git LFS on the Git server.

Install Git LFS on all developer machines.

Configure the Git client to use Git LFS.

Use LFS pointers to replace large files in Git with small pointers.

Use LFS hooks to enforce the LFS policy, automatically convert large files to LFS pointers, and reject commits that violate the policy.

Monitor LFS usage to ensure that the LFS policy is being followed and to identify any potential issues with LFS usage.

Back up LFS objects to ensure that large files can be restored in the event of data loss.

Use LFS filters to automatically convert large files to LFS pointers during Git operations, such as cloning and pulling.

Manage LFS access to ensure that only authorized users have access to large files.

Setting up and managing Git LFS at scale for a large organization involves several best practices, such as defining a LFS policy, using LFS pointers and hooks, monitoring LFS usage, backing up LFS objects, using LFS filters, and managing LFS access. By following these best practices and establishing an effective workflow, organizations can manage large files in Git repositories more efficiently and with greater ease.

6.5 How do you design and enforce policies for commit signing and verification in a large organization?

Commit signing and verification are important security measures that can help ensure the integrity of Git repositories. In a large organization, designing and enforcing policies for commit signing and verification is crucial to maintaining the security of the codebase.

Designing Policies for Commit Signing and Verification

To design policies for commit signing and verification, you will need to consider the following factors:

Signing key management: Determine how signing keys will be managed and stored, and who will have access to them.

Signing requirements: Determine what types of commits require signing and what level of signing is required.

Verification requirements: Determine how commits will be verified and what level of verification is required.

Communication and training: Communicate the policy to all developers and provide training on how to sign and verify commits.

Enforcing Policies for Commit Signing and Verification

To enforce policies for commit signing and verification, you will need to consider the following best practices:

Use pre-commit hooks: Use pre-commit hooks to enforce the signing policy and prevent unsigned commits from being pushed to the repository.

Use post-commit hooks: Use post-commit hooks to verify the authenticity of signed commits and reject those that are not valid.

Use automation tools: Use automation tools, such as continuous integration and deployment pipelines, to automatically sign and verify commits.

Monitor compliance: Monitor compliance with the policy to ensure that all developers are signing and verifying commits as required.

Enforce consequences: Enforce consequences for developers who do not comply with the policy, such as blocking their access to the repository.

Example Workflow

Here is an example workflow for designing and enforcing policies for commit signing and verification in a large organization:

Define a policy for commit signing and verification that includes requirements for signing and verification.

Communicate the policy to all developers and provide training on how to sign and verify commits.

Use pre-commit hooks to enforce the signing policy and prevent unsigned commits from being pushed to the repository.

Use post-commit hooks to verify the authenticity of signed commits and reject those that are not valid.

Use automation tools, such as continuous integration and deployment pipelines, to automatically sign and verify commits.

Monitor compliance with the policy to ensure that all developers are signing and verifying commits as required.

Enforce consequences for developers who do not comply with the policy, such as blocking their access to the repository.

6.6 Can you discuss the internals of Git's transfer protocols (smart HTTP, SSH, Git protocol), and their performance implications?

Git supports several transfer protocols for communicating with remote repositories, including smart HTTP, SSH, and the Git protocol. Each protocol has its own characteristics and performance implications.

Smart HTTP

Smart HTTP is a protocol for Git that allows repositories to be accessed over HTTP or HTTPS. It is called "smart" because it uses the Git protocol to communicate with the server, which allows it to perform faster than traditional HTTP protocols.

Smart HTTP is designed to work well with proxies and firewalls, and is often the preferred

6.7 What are the security concerns and best practices for managing access to a large-scale Git-based infrastructure?

Managing access to a large-scale Git-based infrastructure is critical to maintaining the security of the codebase. In this answer, we will discuss some security concerns and best practices for managing access to such an infrastructure.

Security Concerns

There are several security concerns to consider when managing access to a large-scale Git-based infrastructure:

Authentication: Ensuring that only authorized users have access to the repository is crucial. This can be achieved through various authentication methods such as usernames and passwords, SSH keys, or two-factor authentication.

Authorization: Once a user is authenticated, it is important to ensure that they only have access to the parts of the repository that they need to do their job. This can be done through role-based access control (RBAC) or other access control mechanisms.

Auditing: Tracking and monitoring all access to the repository is important for detecting and preventing unauthorized access or changes to the codebase. This can be achieved through access logs, audit trails, and other monitoring mechanisms.

Code signing: Implementing a code signing policy can help ensure that all changes to the codebase are verified and authorized before they are merged into the main branch.

Best Practices

To manage access to a large-scale Git-based infrastructure securely, consider the following best practices:

Use secure authentication methods: Use secure authentication methods such as SSH keys or two-factor authentication to ensure that only authorized users have access to the repository.

Implement access controls: Implement access controls such as RBAC to ensure that users only have access to the parts of the repository that they need to do their job.

Use strong passwords: Ensure that all user accounts have strong passwords that are changed regularly.

Enforce code signing: Enforce a code signing policy to ensure that all changes to the codebase are verified and authorized before they are merged into the main branch.

Monitor access: Monitor all access to the repository and audit all changes to the codebase to detect and prevent unauthorized access or changes.

Regularly review and update access: Regularly review and update access controls to ensure that only authorized users have access to the repository,

6.8   How do you handle and recover from Git repository corruption, and what are the common causes of corruption?

Git repository corruption can occur due to various reasons such as hardware failure, software bugs, or even human error. In this answer, we will discuss some common causes of Git repository corruption, how to handle and recover from it, and some best practices to prevent it.

Common Causes of Corruption

The following are some common causes of Git repository corruption:

Hardware failure: Hard disk or network issues can cause data loss or corruption.

Software bugs: Bugs in Git or other software used with Git can cause corruption.

Malicious attacks: Malware or other malicious software can corrupt the repository.

Human error: Accidentally deleting or modifying files or directories can cause data loss or corruption.

Handling and Recovering from Corruption

If you suspect that your Git repository is corrupted, the first step is to stop using it immediately to prevent further damage. You can then try the following steps to recover from the corruption:

Check the repository's integrity: Run Git's built-in integrity check using the "git fsck" command. This will check the repository's object database for any inconsistencies or errors.

Restore from backup: If you have a recent backup of the repository, you can restore it to a new location and continue working from there.

Use Git recovery tools: Git provides some built-in tools for recovering from corruption, such as "git reflog" and "git stash". These can help you recover lost commits or other data.

Contact Git support: If the above steps fail, you can contact Git support for assistance in recovering your repository.

Best Practices to Prevent Corruption

The following are some best practices to prevent Git repository corruption:

Regular backups: Regularly back up your repository to ensure that you can restore it if corruption occurs.

Use a version control system: Use a version control system like Git to track changes to your code and protect it from accidental or malicious changes.

Keep software up-to-date: Keep your Git and other software used with Git up-to-date to minimize the risk of bugs or vulnerabilities.

Use RAID or other redundancy: Use redundant storage systems such as RAID to prevent data loss in case of hardware failure.

Use checksums: Use Git's built-in checksums to verify the integrity of your repository.

Train users: Train users on best practices for using Git and preventing data loss or corruption.

Git repository corruption can occur due to various reasons such as hardware failure, software bugs, or human error. To handle and recover from it, you can use Git's built-in integrity check, restore from backup, or use Git recovery tools. To prevent corruption, you can use regular backups, version control, software updates, redundant storage, checksums, and user training.

6.9 Can you discuss techniques for optimizing Git performance, such as reducing repository size, improving network efficiency, and speeding up common operations?

Git is a powerful version control system, but it can be slow when dealing with large repositories or when performing certain operations. In this answer, we will discuss some techniques for optimizing Git performance, including reducing repository size, improving network efficiency, and speeding up common operations.

Reducing Repository Size

One of the most effective ways to improve Git performance is to reduce the size of the repository. Here are some techniques to achieve this:

Remove unnecessary files: Remove any files that are no longer needed or not used frequently from the repository.

Use Git LFS: Use Git LFS to manage large files separately from the repository, reducing the overall size of the repository.

Use Git packfiles: Use Git packfiles to compress the repository's objects and reduce the overall size of the repository.

Use shallow clones: Use shallow clones to clone only the necessary commits, rather than the entire repository history.

Improving Network Efficiency

Git's performance can be impacted by network latency, especially when working with remote repositories. Here are some techniques to improve network efficiency:

Use HTTP/2 or SSH: Use HTTP/2 or SSH to reduce network latency and speed up data transfer.

Use Git protocol: Use the Git protocol, which is designed specifically for Git data transfer, to reduce network latency.

Use a CDN: Use a Content Delivery Network (CDN) to cache frequently accessed data and reduce network latency.

Use compression: Use Git's built-in compression to reduce the size of data transferred over the network.

Speeding up Common Operations

Here are some techniques to speed up common Git operations:

Use Git's built-in caching: Git has a built-in caching mechanism that can improve the performance of frequently used commands.

Use Git's index: Use Git's index to speed up the "git status" and "git add" commands.

Use Git's parallelization: Use Git's parallelization features to speed up operations that can be performed in parallel, such as fetching data from multiple remote repositories simultaneously.

Use Git hooks: Use Git hooks to automate repetitive tasks and reduce the time spent on manual tasks.

Example Workflow

Here is an example workflow for optimizing Git performance:

Remove unnecessary files from the repository to reduce its size.

Use Git LFS to manage large files separately from the repository.

Use Git packfiles to compress the repository's objects and reduce its size.

Use HTTP/2 or SSH to reduce network latency.

Use Git's built-in caching mechanism to speed up frequently used commands.

Use Git's index to speed up "git status" and "git add" commands.

Use Git's parallelization features to speed up operations that can be performed in parallel.

Use Git hooks to automate repetitive tasks and reduce manual work.

Conclusion

Optimizing Git performance is critical to improving the efficiency of development workflows. By reducing repository size, improving network efficiency, and speeding up common operations, developers can save time and increase productivity. Some techniques for achieving this include removing unnecessary files, using Git LFS, using Git packfiles, using HTTP/2 or SSH, using Git's caching and parallelization features, and using Git hooks to automate repetitive tasks.

6.10 How do you set up and manage Git mirroring and replication for high availability and improved performance in a distributed environment?

Git mirroring and replication are techniques used to ensure high availability and improved performance in a distributed environment. In this answer, we will discuss how to set up and manage Git mirroring and replication.

Git Mirroring

Git mirroring is the process of creating a mirror copy of a repository on another server. This can be used to ensure that the repository is available even if the primary server goes down. Here are the steps to set up Git mirroring:

Create a bare clone of the primary repository on the mirror server:

```
git clone --mirror <primary-repo-url>
```

Set up a mirror push to the mirror server:

```
git remote set-url --push origin <mirror-repo-url>
git push --mirror
```

Schedule regular updates to keep the mirror up to date:

```
git remote update
```

Git Replication

Git replication is the process of distributing a repository across multiple servers to improve performance and availability. Here are the steps to set up Git replication:

Create a bare clone of the primary repository on each server:

```
git clone --bare <primary-repo-url>
```

Add the other servers as remotes to the primary repository:

```
git remote add <remote-name> <remote-repo-url>
```

Push to each remote server to replicate the repository:

```
git push --mirror <remote-name>
```

Schedule regular updates to keep the replicas up to date:

```
git remote update
```

Git Mirroring and Replication Best Practices

Here are some best practices for managing Git mirroring and replication:

Use Git hooks to automate the mirroring and replication process.

Use a load balancer to distribute traffic among the replica servers.

Use a monitoring tool to ensure that the replicas are up to date and available.

Use a failover mechanism to switch to a replica server if the primary server goes down.

Use encryption and access controls to ensure the security of the repository.

Git mirroring and replication are important techniques for ensuring high availability and improved performance in a distributed environment. By following the steps outlined above and adopting best practices, developers can set up and manage Git mirroring and replication effectively.

6.11 How do you create and manage custom Git commands and extensions to address unique requirements within an organization?

Git is a powerful tool that can be extended to meet the unique requirements of different organizations. In this answer, we will discuss how to create and manage custom Git commands and extensions.

Creating Custom Git Commands

Git allows you to create custom commands that can be executed using the "git" command-line tool. Here are the steps to create a custom Git command:

Create a Bash script with the custom command:

```
#!/bin/bash

echo "Hello, world!"
```

Make the script executable:

```
chmod +x git-hello-world.sh
```

Add the script to your PATH:

```
export PATH=$PATH:/path/to/git-hello-world.sh
```

Use the custom command:

```
git hello-world
```

Creating Git Extensions

Git extensions are reusable scripts that can be executed using the "git" command-line tool. Here are the steps to create a Git extension:

Create a Bash script with the extension:

```
#!/bin/bash

git log --pretty=format:"%h %s" --topo-order
```

Make the script executable:
```
chmod +x git-topo-order.sh
```

Add the extension to your PATH:
```
export PATH=$PATH:/path/to/git-topo-order.sh
```

Use the Git extension:
```
git topo-order
```

Managing Custom Git Commands and Extensions

Here are some tips for managing custom Git commands and extensions:

Store custom commands and extensions in a central repository.

Use a version control system to manage changes to custom commands and extensions.

Use Git hooks to enforce policies around custom commands and extensions.

Provide documentation and training for custom commands and extensions to ensure that they are used correctly.

Custom Git commands and extensions can be a powerful tool for addressing unique requirements within an organization. By following the steps outlined above and adopting best practices for managing custom Git commands and extensions, organizations can extend Git's capabilities and improve their development workflows.

6.12 Can you discuss techniques for advanced conflict resolution in Git, including resolving complex merge conflicts in large-scale projects?

Git provides several techniques for resolving conflicts that may arise during merging or rebasing. In this answer, we will discuss some advanced techniques for conflict resolution in Git, including resolving complex merge conflicts in large-scale projects.

Understanding Git Conflicts

A conflict occurs in Git when two or more changes to the same file cannot be merged automatically. Git will alert the user to the conflict and ask them to resolve it manually. Conflicts can arise when multiple developers modify the same code simultaneously or when a branch is out of date with the main codebase.

Resolving Conflicts

Here are some techniques for resolving conflicts in Git:

Merge Tool: Git provides a merge tool that can be used to visually compare and merge changes. The user can select which changes to keep and which to discard. Popular merge tools include KDiff3, Beyond Compare, and meld.

Command-Line: The Git command-line tool provides a way to manually resolve conflicts by editing the conflicting files. The user can examine the conflicting changes and decide which changes to keep and which to discard.

Git Rerere: Git Rerere (Reuse Recorded Resolution) is a tool that records conflict resolutions and can automatically apply them in the future. This tool is useful for resolving conflicts that occur repeatedly.

Git Attributes: Git attributes allow developers to specify merge drivers for specific file types. This can be useful for resolving conflicts in binary files, such as images or PDFs.

Resolving Complex Merge Conflicts in Large-Scale Projects

Large-scale projects can be particularly challenging to manage when it comes to resolving merge conflicts. Here are some techniques for resolving complex merge conflicts in large-scale projects:

Use Branching: By creating smaller branches, developers can minimize the scope of conflicts and make them easier to resolve. This also makes it easier to revert changes if necessary.

Use Pull Requests: Pull requests can be used to review changes before they are merged into the main codebase. This can help catch conflicts early and prevent them from causing issues later on.

Use Continuous Integration: Continuous integration tools can be used to automatically build and test code changes, catching conflicts before they are merged into the main codebase.

Use Automated Tools: Automated tools, such as merge bots or conflict resolution scripts, can be used to automatically resolve common conflicts. This can save time and reduce the risk of human error.

Git provides several techniques for resolving conflicts, including using merge tools, the command-line tool, Git Rerere, and Git attributes. Resolving conflicts in large-scale projects can be particularly challenging, but using branching, pull requests, continuous integration, and automated tools can help simplify the process. By adopting these techniques, organizations can minimize the risk of conflicts causing issues and ensure a smooth development process.

6.13 How do you implement and enforce code review policies and practices using Git and Git-based platforms like GitHub, GitLab, or Bitbucket?

Code review is a critical part of the software development process that ensures the quality of the codebase, promotes collaboration among team members, and helps identify potential bugs and vulnerabilities. Git-based platforms like GitHub, GitLab, or Bitbucket provide built-in tools and features to implement and enforce code review policies and practices.

Implementing Code Review Policies and Practices

Here are some steps to implement code review policies and practices using Git-based platforms:

Define Review Criteria: Define the criteria that code should meet to pass the review process, such as adherence to coding standards, proper documentation, and adequate test coverage.

Assign Reviewers: Assign one or more reviewers to the pull request or merge request based on their expertise and availability. It's important to ensure that reviewers are not the same people who wrote the code to avoid bias.

Review Process: The reviewer should review the code, provide feedback, and suggest changes to improve the code quality. The author can then make the suggested changes and resubmit the code for further review. This process may repeat until the code meets the defined criteria.

Approve the Code: Once the code meets the review criteria, the reviewer can approve the code, and it can be merged into the main codebase.

Enforcing Code Review Policies and Practices

Here are some techniques to enforce code review policies and practices using Git-based platforms:

Required Approvals: Git-based platforms allow administrators to require a minimum number of approvals before merging a pull request or merge request. This ensures that code is reviewed by multiple people and reduces the risk of errors.

Branch Protection: Branch protection allows administrators to prevent code from being merged into specific branches without proper code review. This can be used to enforce code review policies and ensure that only high-quality code is merged into the main codebase.

Automated Tools: Automated tools, such as code analysis tools, can be used to check code for adherence to coding standards, proper documentation, and test coverage. These tools can also automatically enforce code review policies by preventing code that does not meet the criteria from being merged.

Best Practices for Code Review

Here are some best practices for code review:

Be Constructive: Provide feedback in a constructive manner and suggest improvements rather than criticizing the code.

Review Small Changes: Review small changes instead of large ones to make the process more manageable and reduce the risk of errors.

Review Often: Review code often to catch issues early in the development process.

Use Checklists: Use checklists to ensure that all review criteria are met, and no critical issues are missed.

Implementing and enforcing code review policies and practices using Git-based platforms like GitHub, GitLab, or Bitbucket is essential for ensuring the quality of the codebase, promoting collaboration among team members, and identifying potential bugs and vulnerabilities. By defining review criteria, assigning reviewers, enforcing code review policies, and following best practices, organizations can ensure that only high-quality code is merged into the main codebase.

6.14 How do you integrate Git with other development tools and platforms, such as continuous integration systems, project management tools, and code review tools?

Git is a widely used version control system that can be integrated with various development tools and platforms to streamline the software development process. Here are some techniques for integrating Git with other development tools and platforms:

Continuous Integration Systems

Continuous Integration (CI) is a software development practice that involves frequently integrating code changes into a shared repository and automatically testing those changes. Git can be integrated with various CI systems like Jenkins, Travis CI, CircleCI, and more to automate the build and test processes.

Here's an example of how to integrate Git with Jenkins:

Set up a Jenkins job to build and test code changes.

Configure the Jenkins job to fetch the code changes from the Git repository using the Git plugin.

Trigger the Jenkins job to run automatically whenever code changes are pushed to the Git repository.

Review the results of the Jenkins job to ensure that the code changes meet the defined criteria.

Project Management Tools

Project management tools like Jira, Trello, and Asana can be integrated with Git to manage tasks, track issues, and monitor progress. This integration allows developers to associate code changes with specific tasks or issues and keep track of the progress of each task or issue.

Here's an example of how to integrate Git with Jira:

Set up a Jira project to manage tasks and issues.

Link the Jira project to the Git repository using the Jira DVCS connector.

Create a new branch in Git for each Jira issue.

Commit code changes to the branch and include the Jira issue key in the commit message.

Use the Jira issue key to track the progress of the issue and monitor the associated code changes.

Code Review Tools

Code review tools like Gerrit, Crucible, and Review Board can be integrated with Git to facilitate code reviews and ensure that code changes meet the defined criteria. This integration allows developers to review code changes, provide feedback, and suggest improvements.

Here's an example of how to integrate Git with Gerrit:

Set up a Gerrit server to manage code reviews.

Configure the Gerrit server to fetch code changes from the Git repository.

Create a new branch in Git for each code review.

Push the code changes to the branch and submit the branch for review using Gerrit.

Review the code changes in Gerrit, provide feedback, and suggest improvements.

Once the code changes meet the review criteria, approve the changes, and merge the branch into the main codebase.

Conclusion

Integrating Git with other development tools and platforms like continuous integration systems, project management tools, and code review tools can improve productivity and efficiency in the software development process. By automating build and test processes, managing tasks and issues, and facilitating code reviews, organizations can ensure that code changes meet the defined criteria and are of high quality.

6.15 How do you manage and enforce branch protection policies in a Git repository to ensure code quality and prevent unintended changes?

Managing and enforcing branch protection policies is an important aspect of ensuring code quality and preventing unintended changes in a Git repository.

In this answer, I will discuss the process of managing and enforcing branch protection policies in a Git repository, including examples of common policies and how to set them up.

Branch Protection Policies

Branch protection policies are rules that dictate who can make changes to a specific branch and how those changes are made. These policies can include requirements for pull request approvals, code reviews, tests, and other quality assurance measures. Branch protection policies can help ensure that changes are made in a controlled and consistent manner, minimizing the risk of errors and security vulnerabilities.

Setting Up Branch Protection Policies

Most Git hosting platforms, including GitHub and GitLab, provide built-in tools for

6.16 Can you discuss strategies for managing Git's configuration settings at the user, repository, and organization levels to enforce best practices?

Git's configuration settings can be managed at three different levels - the user level, the repository level, and the organization level. Here are some strategies for managing Git's configuration settings at each level:

User Level: Git's user-level configuration is stored in the .gitconfig file in the user's home directory. This file contains settings that are specific to the user and are applied to all Git repositories on the user's machine. Here are some strategies for managing Git's configuration settings at the user level:

Use a template .gitconfig file: Organizations can provide a template .gitconfig file that contains recommended settings for all users to use. This file can be stored in a shared location, and all users can copy it to their home directory and customize it as needed.

Use aliases: Git aliases can be used to create shortcuts for frequently used commands. Organizations can provide a set of aliases for users to use, which can help enforce consistency and improve productivity.

Enforce global configuration settings: Git allows users to set global configuration settings that are applied to all Git repositories on their machine. Organizations can enforce certain global configuration settings to ensure that best practices are followed. For example, an organization might enforce the use of a specific text editor for commit messages.

Repository Level: Git's repository-level configuration is stored in the .git/config file in the root directory of the repository. This file contains settings that are specific to the repository and are applied only to that repository. Here are some strategies for managing Git's configuration settings at the repository level:

Use a template config file: Organizations can provide a template .git/config file that contains recommended settings for all repositories to use. This file can be stored in a shared location, and all repositories can copy it to their root directory and customize it as needed.

Use hooks: Git hooks can be used to enforce certain behaviors or checks before and after certain Git commands are executed. Organizations can provide a set of hooks that enforce best practices, such as checking for the presence of a certain file before committing changes.

Enforce repository-specific settings: Git allows repository-specific configuration settings to be applied via the .git/config file. Organizations can enforce certain repository-specific settings to ensure that best practices are followed. For example, an organization might enforce the use of a specific merge strategy for a particular repository.

Organization Level: Git's organization-level configuration is stored in a file called gitconfig in the .git/ directory of the organization's root directory. This file contains settings that are specific to the organization and are applied to all repositories within that organization. Here are some strategies for managing Git's configuration settings at the organization level:

Use a template gitconfig file: Organizations can provide a template gitconfig file that contains recommended settings for all repositories within the organization to use. This file can be stored in a shared location, and all repositories can copy it to their .git/ directory and customize it as needed.

Use Git submodules: Git submodules can be used to include one Git repository as a subdirectory of another Git repository. Organizations can use submodules to enforce the use of certain repositories or components across all repositories within the organization.

Enforce organization-wide settings: Git allows organization-wide configuration settings to be applied via the gitconfig file in the .git/ directory. Organizations can enforce certain organization-wide settings to ensure that best practices are followed. For example, an organization might enforce the use of a specific branch naming convention for all repositories within the organization.

In summary, managing Git's configuration settings at different levels requires a combination of providing recommended templates

6.17 How do you manage and recover from issues with Git submodules or subtrees in a large-scale project?

Managing Git submodules and subtrees can be a challenging task, especially in large-scale projects where there are many contributors and multiple repositories involved. Here are some best practices for managing and recovering from issues with Git submodules or subtrees:

Understand the difference between submodules and subtrees: Submodules and subtrees are two different ways of incorporating one repository into another. Submodules are a separate Git repository that is embedded within another Git repository at a specific path, while subtrees are a part of another Git repository that is kept in sync with a separate repository.

Use descriptive commit messages: It's essential to use descriptive commit messages when working with submodules or subtrees to make it easier to track changes and understand what is happening within the repository. Clear commit messages can help to diagnose and recover from issues.

Always keep track of the latest version of submodules or subtrees: Make sure to keep track of the latest version of submodules or subtrees to avoid conflicts and ensure that changes are properly synced between the repositories.

Use the appropriate Git commands: Use Git commands such as git submodule update or git subtree pull to keep submodules or subtrees in sync. Also, ensure that you use the appropriate commands when working with submodules or subtrees, such as git submodule init and git submodule add for submodules, and git subtree add for subtrees.

Test before committing changes: Before committing changes to submodules or subtrees, make sure to test them thoroughly to avoid introducing issues that may be difficult to recover from. This includes checking that the submodule or subtree is still working as expected after changes have been made.

Create backups: Creating backups of submodules or subtrees can be helpful in case of unexpected issues or data loss. This can be done by copying the submodule or subtree directory to another location or using Git commands like git clone to create a copy of the repository.

If issues do arise, here are some steps to help recover from them:

Check Git logs: Git logs can be helpful in diagnosing issues with submodules or subtrees. Use git log –submodule or git log –oneline to view a summary of commits that have been made to submodules or subtrees.

Use Git commands to revert changes: Git commands like git revert or git reset can be used to revert changes that have been made to submodules or subtrees.

Update submodules or subtrees: Use Git commands like git submodule update or git subtree pull to update submodules or subtrees to their latest version.

Restore from backups: If backups have been created, they can be used to restore submodules or subtrees to their previous state.

Overall, managing and recovering from issues with Git submodules or subtrees in a large-scale project requires attention to detail, clear communication between contributors, and proper use of Git commands.

6.18 How do you troubleshoot and resolve performance issues with Git operations, such as slow clone, fetch, or push operations?

Troubleshooting and resolving performance issues with Git operations can be challenging, especially in large repositories or when working with remote repositories. Here are some best practices for troubleshooting and resolving performance issues with Git operations:

Identify the root cause: The first step in troubleshooting Git performance issues is to identify the root cause. This could be due to network issues, the size of the repository, or other factors. One way to identify the root cause is to run Git commands with the -v or –verbose flag, which can provide more information about what is happening during the operation.

Check network performance: Slow Git operations can often be caused by network issues. To check network performance, use tools like ping or traceroute to identify network latency or packet loss issues. It may also be helpful to check with your internet service provider (ISP) or network administrator to see if there are any known issues.

Optimize Git configuration: Git has several configuration options that can be used to optimize performance, such as increasing the buffer size or setting a higher compression level. These options can be set using the git config command. For example, to increase the buffer size, you can use git config –global http.postBuffer 524288000.

Reduce repository size: Large repository sizes can cause slow Git operations. To reduce the repository size, consider removing large files or using Git's built-in tools for managing large files, such as Git LFS (Large File Storage).

Use shallow clones: Shallow clones can be used to reduce the amount of data that needs to be transferred during clone operations. This can be done using the –depth option with the git clone command. For example, to clone a repository with a depth of 1, use git clone –depth 1 <repository URL>.

Use Git hooks: Git hooks can be used to automate tasks that can slow down Git operations. For example, pre-commit hooks can be used to check for syntax errors or run tests before committing changes, which can prevent large numbers of failed commits that could slow down Git operations.

Use Git's built-in caching: Git has a built-in caching mechanism that can speed up operations by caching objects and references. This can be done using the git gc command or by setting the gc.auto configuration option.

If performance issues persist, there are a few other options that can be considered:

Use a Git hosting service: Git hosting services like GitHub, GitLab, and Bitbucket offer optimized infrastructure and caching mechanisms that can improve Git performance.

Consider using a distributed file system: Distributed file systems like NFS or GlusterFS can be used to store Git repositories, which can improve performance by distributing the workload across multiple servers.

Consider using a Git proxy server: Git proxy servers like GitProxy can be used to cache Git operations and reduce the load on the Git server.

Overall, troubleshooting and resolving performance issues with Git operations requires a combination of identifying the root cause, optimizing Git configuration, reducing repository size, using Git hooks, and using Git's built-in caching. By following these best practices, it is possible to improve Git performance and reduce the time required for common Git operations.

6.19 How do you handle and mitigate security vulnerabilities in Git itself and Git-based platforms like GitHub, GitLab, or Bitbucket?

Handling and mitigating security vulnerabilities in Git and Git-based platforms like GitHub, GitLab, or Bitbucket is critical to ensure the safety and integrity of code repositories. Here are some best practices for handling and mitigating security vulnerabilities:

Keep Git and Git-based platforms up to date: Keeping Git and Git-based platforms up to date with the latest security patches and updates is essential to mitigate security vulnerabilities. This includes regularly checking for updates and security advisories and promptly applying any updates or patches.

Use secure authentication methods: Using secure authentication methods, such as SSH or two-factor authentication, can help to prevent unauthorized access to repositories. It's also important to ensure that passwords are complex and regularly changed.

Use access controls: Access controls can be used to limit access to repositories and prevent unauthorized users from making changes. This includes using user roles and permissions, setting branch protection rules, and limiting access to certain IP addresses or networks.

Implement code review processes: Code review processes can help to identify and mitigate security vulnerabilities by allowing other developers to review code changes before they are committed to the repository.

Use vulnerability scanning tools: Vulnerability scanning tools can be used to identify potential security vulnerabilities in code repositories. These tools can scan for known vulnerabilities in third-party dependencies, identify misconfigurations, and check for insecure code practices.

Use Git hooks for security checks: Git hooks can be used to perform security checks on code changes before they are committed to the repository. This includes checking for secrets, preventing large files from being committed, and running tests to check for security vulnerabilities.

Monitor for suspicious activity: Monitoring for suspicious activity, such as unusual login attempts or changes to access controls, can help to identify potential security breaches early and prevent further damage.

If a security vulnerability is identified, here are some steps to take to mitigate the issue:

Patch the vulnerability: If a security vulnerability is identified in Git or a Git-based platform, it's essential to promptly apply any available patches or updates to mitigate the issue.

Notify affected users: If a security vulnerability has the potential to impact users, it's important to notify them as soon as possible so they can take appropriate measures to protect themselves.

Review code changes: If a security vulnerability is identified in a repository, it's important to review recent code changes to identify any potential sources of the vulnerability and take appropriate action.

Revoke access: If unauthorized access is suspected, it's important to immediately revoke access to prevent further damage.

Overall, handling and mitigating security vulnerabilities in Git and Git-based platforms requires a combination of preventive measures, such as keeping software up to date and using secure authentication methods, and reactive measures, such as patching vulnerabilities and monitoring for suspicious activity. By following these best practices, it is possible to mitigate security vulnerabilities and protect code repositories.

6.20 What are the challenges and best practices for managing Git repositories in a geographically distributed team or organization?

Managing Git repositories in a geographically distributed team or organization can be challenging, but there are several best practices that can help ensure smooth collaboration and effective management. Here are some of the key challenges and best practices:

Challenges:

Network and connectivity issues: Geographically distributed teams may face issues with network connectivity, which can slow down Git operations or cause data loss.

Time zone differences: Teams in different time zones may have difficulty collaborating effectively or coordinating their work.

Communication barriers: Teams may have difficulty communicating effectively due to language or cultural differences, as well as differences in communication styles.

Branch and repository management: Geographically distributed teams may face challenges with branch and repository management, such as keeping repositories in sync and resolving conflicts.

Best practices:

Use a centralized Git hosting service: Using a centralized Git hosting service, such as GitHub, GitLab, or Bitbucket, can help ensure that repositories are easily accessible to all team members and provide a centralized location for collaboration.

Use Git workflows: Using Git workflows, such as Gitflow or GitHub flow, can help ensure that code changes are reviewed and tested before being merged into the main repository.

Use pull requests: Pull requests can help facilitate code reviews and ensure that changes are properly tested before being merged into the main repository.

Use issue trackers: Issue trackers, such as Jira or GitHub Issues, can help teams track and prioritize tasks and ensure that work is properly coordinated across the team.

Use chat or video conferencing tools: Chat or video conferencing tools, such as Slack or Zoom, can help teams communicate effectively and collaborate in real time.

Use automation tools: Automation tools, such as continuous integration and deployment (CI/CD) tools or Git hooks, can help automate routine tasks and ensure that code changes are properly tested and deployed.

Use code reviews: Code reviews can help ensure that changes are properly reviewed and tested before being merged into the main repository, and can also help identify potential issues or vulnerabilities.

Document best practices: Documenting best practices, such as coding standards or Git workflows, can help ensure that all team members are on the same page and can effectively collaborate across geographic boundaries.

Overall, managing Git repositories in a geographically distributed team or organization requires a combination of communication, collaboration, and effective use of Git workflows and tools. By following these best practices, it is possible to effectively manage Git repositories and ensure that teams are able to collaborate effectively across geographic boundaries.

Made in the USA
Monee, IL
08 January 2025

76352779R00075